So You're Getting Married

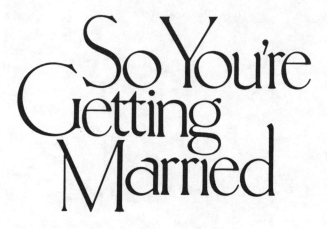

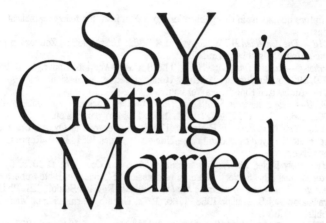

So You're Getting Married

H. Norman Wright
Author of Best-selling
COMMUNICATION: KEY TO YOUR MARRIAGE

Regal Books
A Division of GL Publications
Ventura, California, U.S.A.

Rights for publishing this book in other languages are contracted by Gospel Literature International (GLINT) foundation. GLINT also provides technical help for the adaptation, translation, and publishing of Bible study resources and books in scores of languages worldwide. For further information, contact GLINT, Post Office Box 6688, Ventura, California 93006, U.S.A., or the publisher.

Published by Regal Books
A Division of GL Publications
Ventura, California 93006
Printed in U.S.A.

Library of Congress Cataloging in Publication Data

Wright, H. Norman.
  So you're getting married.

  Bibliography: p.
    1. Marriage—Religious aspects—Christianity.
2. Marriage.   3. Communication in marriage.   I. Title.
II. Title: So you are getting married.
BV835.W745   1985   248.4   85-18364
ISBN 0-8307-1095-7

The material in this book is selected or adapted from the following books by H. Norman Wright:
Communication: Key to Your Marriage
More Communication Keys for Your Marriage
The Pillars of Marriage
Seasons of a Marriage
For the sake of easier reading, the use of *fiancé* in this book refers to both males and females.

CONTENTS

1
COMMITMENT TO MARRIAGE

Why are you getting married? What are your dreams, expectations and hopes for the future? What part does marriage play in those dreams and hopes? How do you look at marriage? What do you expect from your marriage? Your answer might include one or more of the following statements:

"I want to share my life with someone."

"I want someone to help make me happy."

"I want to spend my life with someone I love and with someone who loves me."

"I don't want to spend my life alone."

"I want to make up for all that was lacking in my own home."

"I want to be faithful to God and love someone He wants me to love."

"I don't want to end up alone, especially when I get older. Marriage is a security."

"I want the security of a permanent relationship."

All of these are fringe benefits of marriage, but none is strong enough to stand as a foundation for marriage.

Many people are propelled toward marriage without really understanding all they are committing themselves to for the rest of their lives. That is why couples experience surprises and upsets throughout the duration of their marriages. Marriage is many things.

Marriage is a gift.

Marriage is an opportunity for love to be learned.

Marriage is a journey in which we as the travelers are faced with many choices and are responsible for these choices.

Marriage is affected more by our inner communication than our outer communication.

Marriage is more often influenced by unresolved issues from our past than we realize.

Marriage is a call to servanthood.

Marriage is a call to friendship.

Marriage is a call to suffering.

Marriage is a refining process. It is an opportunity to be refined by God into the person He wants us to be.

Marriage is not an event but a way of life.

Marriage involves intimacy in all areas for it to be fulfilling.

Marriage Is a Commitment

I would like to ask you a basic question. Only you will know the real answer but your response may determine whether marriage is for you at this time of your life.

Are you ready for a commitment? Face your partner. Look at that person and hold his or her hand. You are committing yourself to about 50 years with that individual. Think about it! It is important to think twice before entering a room with no exits. You cannot have complete liberty and commitment. You cannot be married and single. Becoming two means you are no longer just one. The commitment holds true even during a short-term or life-long illness, poverty, a lawsuit, loss of job, a handicapped child or any other of life's surprises.

Please do not marry if you cannot keep a commitment. Marriage is an unconditional commitment and not a contract. Some psychologists, marriage counselors and ministers have suggested that marriage is a contract, and many people are quick to agree. But is this really true? Is marriage really a contract?

In every contract there are certain conditional clauses. A contract between two parties, whether they be companies or individuals, involves the responsibility of both parties to carry out their part of the bargain. These are conditional clauses or "if" clauses. If you do this, the other person must do this, and if the other person does this, you must do this. But in the marriage relationship there are no conditional clauses. Nowhere in the marriage ceremony does the pastor say, "If the husband loves his wife then the wife continues in the contract." Or, "If the wife is submissive to her husband then the husband carries out the contract." Marriage is an unconditional commitment into which two people enter.

In most contracts there are escape clauses. An escape clause says that if the party of the first part does not carry out his responsibilities, then the party of the second part is absolved. If one person does not live up to his part of the bargain, the second person can get out of the contract. This is an escape clause. In marriage there is no escape clause.

Unfortunately, many people *do* enter marriage with an attitude that there is an escape clause—if they do not get along they can break the relationship and try again. Too many are impatient with their marriages. They do not want to live "happily ever after." They want to live happily right away or else! As a young wife sitting in a marriage counselor's office said, "When I got married I was looking for an ideal, I married an ordeal, I now want a new deal!" Changing partners is not an option for a Christian. Our calling is to be committed.

Commitment means many things to different people. For some, the strength of their commitment varies with how they feel emotionally or physically. The word "commit" is a verb and means, "to do or to perform." It is a binding pledge or promise. It is a private pledge you also make public. It is a pledge carried out to completion, running over any roadblocks. It is a total giving of oneself to another person. Yes, it is risky, but it makes life fulfilling.

Whereas courtship is a process of selecting the one you are going to commit yourself to, the marriage ceremony is a public act of that commitment. And each day of your marriage you should renew your act of commitment to your marriage partner. Commitment can carry a relationship and keep it alive when the romantic feelings are at a low ebb. One friend said, "I don't always feel romantic or have an overwhelming love response to

her, but I am committed to her, committed to love her for life!"

Commitment involves action. Many couples make a genuine commitment at the altar but their commitment is not lived out in action. For 18 years I have taught at a seminary. Unfortunately, I have seen a number of students put their marriage on the shelf until they graduate. People do this for many reasons, but during that time-out the marriage can die.

You must constantly fight to keep your commitment to marriage primary in your lives and resist the pressure to share that commitment with other facets of life. Your level of commitment is the most vital factor in determining the success or failure of your relationship.

The Word of God indicates that the marriage commitment is both holy and practical. God used the marriage relationship to describe His relationship with the Church—His Bride. He is committed to love her unconditionally. Our marriage vows—our commitment to each other—are very important to Him (see Eph. 5:21-31; Rev. 22:17; Matt. 9:15).

A Christian marriage is a commitment involving three individuals—husband, wife and Jesus Christ. It is a pledge of mutual fidelity and mutual submission. It is an opportunity for each one to grow and develop his or her individual abilities or giftedness.

If you have difficulty following through with commitment, if you are changeable or live according to your emotions, how do you know that you will keep this most important life commitment? There are ways your commitment can last:

1. Daily recommit yourself to your marriage.
2. Allow God the opportunity to help you sustain your commitment.
3. Never neglect or take for granted your marriage. Renew or make it fresh each day.
4. Take definite and specific steps to reach the dreams and goals you have for your marriage.

Before ever starting out on a journey, a wise driver will try to determine what he is most likely to encounter along the way. How are the roads? Will there be any detours? What will the weather be like? If he can know some of these things ahead of time he will be better prepared when he gets to a place where his progress could be hampered without his foreknowledge.

Life's journey has a beginning and some type of conclusion. The time between these two points is a transition. Its events follow a basic sequence and progression—sometimes smooth and orderly, other times rough and bumpy. Marriage is one of the most difficult and complex of these transitions. It is a cooperative venture in which two people are developing a oneness and at the same time maintaining and enhancing their own individuality and potential. It is a journey that involves choosing between numerous paths. Each path has its own characteristics and destinations, some good and some not. It is a journey in which we encounter stages or periods that we might call seasons.

Marriage is one of God's greatest schools of learning—it can be a place where a husband and wife are refined. The rough edges are gradually filed away until there is a deeper, smoother and more fulfilling working and blending together that is satisfying to both individuals.

Why Get Married?

As most couples move toward marriage, their sense of reality is distorted by wishfulness and fantasy, and this intense romantic illusion can neutralize the positive development of their marriage. Unrealistic expectations and fantasies create a gulf between the partners and cause disappointments. Each person in the relationship can create such detailed fantasies that neither the other partner nor the relationship has any chance for survival.

Many marriages today are like the house built upon sand—they have been built upon a weak foundation of dreams. When we dream our minds do not have to distinguish between reality or fantasy, so we are able to create without restraint. Often, therefore, our dreams are starting points for successful endeavors; however, dreams that are not followed by adequate planning usually do not come true.

Marriages built on dreams are risky because dreams do not consider the disappointment and changes that are inevitable in every marriage. When the season changes and the rains of reality and the winds of stress blow upon such marriages, the relationship that *should* hold them together crumbles. Much more is involved in fulfilling dreams than merely expecting them to come true.

Building a good marriage means that you must take time to redefine roles, beliefs and behaviors and negotiate the differences with your partner. Use of space in the home, time, money, power, family traditions, rituals, friends and vocations are just a few of the issues which you will negotiate.

A newly married couple needs a spirit of adventure, because getting married to a "stranger" means that there are going to be a lot of discoveries. What if one is a night person and the other a morning person? One is talkative in the morning and one at night. One likes to be babied when he or she is sick while the other hides illness and wants space at that time. One likes the room at 78 degrees and the other at 68 degrees. One wears a set of underwear for three days; the other changes it twice a day. One uses a towel once and discards it; the other uses it for a week. These are just a few of the practical day-to-day items that can drive a couple crazy. The spirit of adventure will help the couple realize, "We're different and that's OK."

Statistics prove that the prospects of your having a successful marriage are not very encouraging. I see three reasons why marriages dissolve.

First, one or both persons fail to understand the stages and changes of individual development—the seasons of their lives— and how these affect their marriage.

Second, people have an inadequate basis upon which they build their personal identity and security. The best basis for marriage comes from the one who instituted marriage in the first place; but for many, the teachings of God's Word have not been incorporated in depth into their lives, transforming both their identity and their security.

Third, some marriages dissolve because the partners were never prepared for marriage and because their expectations about marriage were totally unrealistic. David Mace, a pioneer in the field of marriage enrichment, describes this lack of preparation:

When I try to reconstruct, in counseling with couples, their concepts of the making of a marriage, I find that it adds up to a most confused hodgepodge of starry-eyed romanticism, superstition, superficial concepts, and laissez-faire. Seldom do I find any real understanding of the complexity of the task of bringing two separate individuals into a delicately balanced coordination of each other's thoughts, feelings, wishes, beliefs, and habit patterns.[1]

Why do people marry? What are the underlying subtle reasons for love? What background influences are somewhat hidden from view? There are numerous reasons for marriage apart from being in love.

Both men and women marry to be taken care of. Some view marriage as a safety net into which they gladly fall. They either see or imagine strength in the other person. If the strength is shared and passed back and forth, intimacy can develop. But if the desire of one partner is for "continuous care," growth is limited.

Pregnancy is still a reason for marriage. In fact, about one-fourth of all marriages occur when the bride is pregnant. Probably many of these marriages would not have occurred had the woman not been pregnant. Research on these marriages shows a relationship between a premarital pregnancy and unhappiness in marriage.[2] In God's grace, these marriages do not have to end or have a greater rate of unhappiness than others; the forgiveness of Jesus Christ can affect this situation as well as any other.

Rebound is a reason for marriage when a person attempts to find a marriage partner immediately after a relationship terminates. In a sense, it is a frantic attempt to establish desirability in the eyes of the person who terminated the relationship. Marriage on the rebound is questionable because the marriage occurs in reference to the previous man or woman and not in reference to the new person.

Rebellion is a motivation for marriage and occurs in both secular and Christian homes. In this situation the parents say no and the young person says yes. This is a demonstration of one's control over one's own life and possibly an attempt to demonstrate independence. Unfortunately, the person uses the marriage partner to get back at his or her parents.

Escape from an unhappy home environment is another reason for marriage. Some of the reasons given are fighting, drinking and molestation. This type of marriage is risky, as the knot-tying is often accomplished before genuine feelings of mutual trust, respect and mature love have had any opportunity to develop.

Loneliness is a reason for marriage that stands by itself. Some cannot bear the thought of remaining alone for the rest of their days; yet they do not realize that a person can be married and still feel terribly lonely. Instantaneous intimacy does not occur at the altar but must be developed over months and years of sharing and involvement. The flight from loneliness may place a strain upon the relationship. One person may be saying, "I'm so lonely. Be with me all the time and make me happy."

Physical appearance influences everyone to some degree yet some marry because they are physically attracted to one another. Our society is highly influenced by the cult of youth and beauty. Often our standards for a partner's physical appearance are set not so much to satisfy our needs, but simply to gain approval and admiration from others. Some build their self-concept upon their partner's physical attributes.

Social pressure may be a direct or indirect reason for marrying and can come from many sources. Friends, parents, churches and schools can convey the message, "It is normal to be married; to fit the norm you should get with it." On some college campuses a malady known as "senior panic" occurs when students make hasty decisions to marry. Engagement and marriage may be a means of gaining status; fears of being left behind are reinforced by others. In some churches when a young unmarried pastor arrives, matchmaking becomes the order of the day. Some churches will not hire a minister unless he is married; thus a young minister must either marry before he is ready to or desires to or spend months looking for a church that will accept a single pastor.

Guilt and pity are still catalysts for some marriages. Marrying a person because one feels sorry for him or her because of physical defects, illness or a poor lot in life does not make a stable marital relationship.

Many actually marry their own physical and emotional need. They have a personal need to be cared for, to be happy, to have economic security, to become a parent, etc. Need fulfillment is important. But these people create an image of a person they think will be able to meet these needs; then they marry their invented image.

Marriage Can Meet Your Needs

God wants your marriage to meet your individual needs. John Lavender, in his book *Marriage at Its Best,* cites seven needs from the Word of God that Christian marriage is designed to meet: completion; consolation; communication; coition; creation; correlation and Christianization.[3]

Completion

In Genesis 2:18 and 24 God says, "It is not good for the man to be alone; I will make him a helper suitable for him . . . . For this cause a man shall leave his father and his mother, and shall cleave to his wife; and they shall become one flesh" *(NASB).* From this passage we understand that marriage brings about completion. Marriage involves a mysterious merging of two separate but equal individuals in such a way that they learn to complement each other and thereby actually complete each other.

We need to remember that the word here is "completion," not "competition." Completion means that fellowship and companionship is involved. But most of all, completion involves friendship.

A friend is a person with whom you feel comfortable. A friend is an individual whose company you prefer over another's. This type of person is someone you can count on—not just for support and encouragement but for out-and-out honesty.

A true friend is an individual who believes in you. He/she shares some of the same beliefs about your potential, your dreams, your concerns. You want to spend all of your life with him/her.

Galatians 6:2 *(NASB)* says, "Bear one another's burdens" and a friend takes this verse seriously. When you hurt, your friend hurts. When you share your concerns and your hurts with him/her, the pain is eased. A friend is someone who gives you safety and trust. You know that what you share will stop right there. It will never be used against you.

Laughter is a part of friendship, but laughter with you, not at you. Praying is a part of friendship too—praying for each other and praying with each other.

A friend is an individual with whom you can share your ideas, your beliefs and your philosophies; and you can grow together intellectually. This may not mean that you have the same level of intelligence or the same educational background, but you find a similarity between you, and you share it together. A friend is one who stands by you in a time of difficulty and trouble, while maintaining a level of objectivity.

Another way of describing a friend is to say that he/she is a person with whom you can be yourself. You can be totally exposed and open. A friend is someone who can see you at your worst as well as at your best, and still love you just the same.

Are you experiencing this kind of relationship at the present time with your fiancé? Could this area of your life be improved? Do the two of you have the potential for this? List three ways you've experienced this kind of friendship up to this point.

1.
2.
3.

Completion is a process, taking work and effort.

Consolation

A second need that is fulfilled in marriage is consolation. Genesis 2:18 *(NASB)* states: "I will make him a helper suitable for him." Consolation comes from speaking in a manner that encourages, supports and brings about healing to the other person. A married individual has the opportunity of being used by God as a channel of His healing grace.

Proverbs 12:25 *(AMP)* puts it this way: "Anxiety in a man's heart weighs it down, but an encouraging word makes it glad."

Proverbs 25:11 *(AMP)* says, "A word fitly spoken and in due season is like apples of gold in a setting of silver."

List three ways you encourage your fiancé.

1.

2.

3.

Are these ways your fiancé would like to be encouraged?

Communication

God also designed Christian marriage for communication. Communication is the means by which one person has the opportunity to learn to know and understand his/her mate. David and Vera Mace liken communication to a large house with many rooms to which a couple fall heir on their wedding day.

> Their hope is to use and enjoy these rooms, as we do the rooms in a comfortable home, so that they will serve the many activities that make up their shared life. But in many marriages doors are found to be locked— they represent areas in the relationship that the couple are unable to explore together. Attempts to open these doors lead to failure and frustration. The right key cannot be found. So the couple resigns themselves to living together in only a few rooms which can be opened easily, leaving the rest of the house with all its promising possibilities unexplored and unused. There is, however, a master key that will open every door. It is not easy to find. Or, more correctly, it has to be forged by the couple together, and this can be very difficult. It is the great art of effective marital communication.[4]

Coition

Yet another need fulfilled in marriage is coition or sexual fulfillment. Sexuality is our celebration of God's continuing creativity. God chose to demonstrate His creative activity in conception of new persons through the intimate act of love union. He has honored the simple act of joining bodies with the ultimate significance of beginning life.

Two who give themselves to each other in the intimacy of marriage celebrate the eternal potential of their act of love. This awareness of its creative meaning gives character to sexual union, even when it is meant as an act of joyous communion with no intention of conception. Then, too, it is a celebration of His creation.[5]

Creation

Another need that can be satisfied with marriage is creation, bringing a new life into being. Dr. Lavender put it this way: "When you and your mate give yourselves to each other in the intimacy of Christian marriage, you not only celebrate your oneness in Spirit, but by the simple act of joining bodies, become participants of God in the continuum of life."[6]

Correlation

Another purpose for marriage is correlation. Correlation has to do with the relationships that exist in a Christian home. Unfortunately, in many marriages we have, instead of a Christian home, a home full of Christians.

The husband and wife relationship and family life is a microcosm of the Body of Christ. It is a little church, a fellowship of believers together. This relationship, particularly between husband and wife, should reflect to others—the non-Christian community—what a church is really like A marriage and a family should be a church in miniature.

> Speaking the truth in love, we are to grow up in all aspects into Him, who is the head, even Christ, from whom the whole body, being fitted and held together by that which every joint supplies, according to the proper working of each individual part, causes the growth of the body for the building up of itself in love (Eph. 4:15-16, *NASB*).

Christianization_____

The ffinal need that is fulfilled in marriage is Christianization. This surprises many couples. A Christian family can be one of the most powerful and persuasive evangelistic forces on earth. However, many Christian marriages do not reflect the reality of the presence of Christ. Living the Christian life in a family is difficult, but it has a far greater effect upon the world than preaching or the distribution of tracts. The Christian family, in a sense, is a proof of the reality of the power of God in an individual's life.

Let me expand a bit more upon what your marriage involves.

Marriage Is a Gift

Marriage is a gift. You may be the finest gift your spouse has ever received! Your spouse may be the finest gift you have received.

A gift is an item which is selected with care and consideration. Its purpose is to bring delight and fulfillment to another, an expression of deep feeling on the part of the giver.

Think of the care and effort you put into selecting a gift. You wonder what the recipient would enjoy. What will bring him/her delight? What will bring happiness? What will make his/her day bright and cheery? What will show the person the extent of your feeling for him/her and how much the person means to you?

Because you want this gift to be special and meaningful you spend time thinking about what gift to select. Then you begin the search through various stores and shops, considering and rejecting several items until the right one beckons to you and you make the selection. You invest time wrapping the gift. You think of how best to present it to the person so his/her delight and pleasure will be heightened.

There is an excitement and a challenge involved in selecting and presenting a special gift. You not only have given the object, you also have given your time and energy. Gifts that are often appreciated the most are not those that are the most expensive, but those which reflect the investment of yourself in considering the desires and wants of the other person. The way you present it and the sacrifice you make also make a gift special.

You are a gift to your spouse. If you consider yourself a gift, how will you live so your spouse feels that he/she has been given a special gift? Will you invest your time, thought and energy in your spouse? Will your spouse experience delight, fulfillment and a feeling of being special? How can you, as a gift, be used in the life of your spouse to lift his/her spirits and outlook on life?

On the receiving end of the gift, how do you react when you receive a special gift that brings you delight? Think of your childhood years. What was the most exciting or special gift you ever received? Can you remember your thoughts and feelings as you received that gift? How did you treat that gift? Did you take special care of it and protect it from harm and loss? Perhaps you gave the gift a special place of prominence and were carefully possessive of it.

If your spouse is a special gift to you, how will you treat this gift? Will you be careful to give your spouse the finest care, attention, protection and place of prominence in your life? Will your partner feel as though he/she really is a gift to you?

A gift is given as an expression of our love. It is not based on whether the recipient deserves it or not. Our giving of a gift is actually an act of grace.

Marriage Is Servanthood

Marriage is a call to servanthood. This is not a very popular concept and not high on the list of priorities for most marriages. We would rather be served than to serve. But our guideline for a Christian marriage is given to us from the Scriptures. Look at the following passages:

> Do not merely look out for your own personal interests, but also for the interests of others. Have this attitude in yourselves which was also in Christ Jesus, who, although He existed in the form of God, did not regard equality with God a thing to be grasped, but emptied Himself, taking the form of a bond-servant, and being made in the likeness of men. And being found in appear-

ance as a man, He humbled Himself by becoming obedi-
ent to the point of death, even death on a cross. Therefore also God highly exalted Him, and bestowed on Him
the name which is above every name (Phil. 2:4-9,
NASB).

Jesus voluntarily submitted to becoming a "bond-servant,"
looking out for our interests rather than His own. In the same
way the Apostle Paul tells us to "be subject to one another in the
fear of Christ" (Eph. 5:21, *NASB*).

Notice one important point: We must never *demand* that our
partner be our servant or live up to the clear teachings of Scripture. If we feel that we have to demand it, or even mention it,
then we become more concerned with meeting our own needs
than with being a servant. If a man has to demand that his wife
see him as the head of the family, then—to be blunt—he has lost
it! Ephesians 5:22-25 says that for a man to be the head he must
love his wife as Christ loved the Church and gave Himself for
her. This means sacrificial love—servanthood.

A truly loving husband will regard his wife as a completely equal partner in everything that concerns their
life together. He will assert his headship to see that this
equal partnership is kept inviolable. Hers is to be an
equal contribution in areas, say, of decision-making,
conflict-resolution, emerging family developmental
planning, and daily family management. Whether it concerns finances, or child discipline, or social life—whatever it may be, she is an equal partner. Loving headship
affirms, defers, shares; it encourages and stimulates.
Loving headship delights to delegate without demanding. Yet, throughout the equalitarian process, the husband knows all the while that he bears the responsibility
before God for the healthful maintenance of the marriage.[7]

To put it simply, a servant's role is to make sure that the
other person's needs are met. In a husband-wife relationship,

being a servant is an act of love, a gift to the other person to make his/her life fuller. It is not something to be demanded. It is an act of strength and not of weakness. It is a positive action which has been chosen to show your love to each other. Hence, the apostle Paul said, "Be subject to one another," not limiting the role of servanthood to the wife.

A servant may also be called an "enabler." The word enable means "to make better." As an enabler you are to make life easier for your spouse instead of placing restrictive demands upon him/her. An enabler does not make more work for the partner, nor does he/she hinder the other from becoming all he/she has been designed to become.

A servant is also one who "edifies" or builds up the other person. The English word edify is derived from the Latin word *aedes* meaning "hearth" or "fireplace." The hearth was the center of activity in ancient times. It was the only place of warmth and light in the home, and the place where the daily bread was prepared. It was also the place where people were drawn together.

Edifying is often used in the New Testament to refer to building up another person. Three examples of edifying are expressed in the verses below: (1) personal encouragement, (2) inner strengthening, and (3) the establishment of peace and harmony between individuals.

"So let us then definitely aim for and eagerly pursue what makes for harmony and for mutual upbuilding (edification and development) of one another" (Rom. 14:19, *AMP*).

"Let each one of us make it a practice to please (make happy) his neighbor for his good and for his true welfare, to edify him—that is, to strengthen him and build him up spiritually" (Rom. 15:2, *AMP*).

"Therefore encourage one another and build each other up, just as in fact you are doing" (1 Thess. 5:11, *NIV*).

First Corinthians 8:1 *(NIV)* sums up the matter of edifying: "Love builds up."

To edify then, means to cheer another person on in life. You are to be a one-person rooting section for your spouse which can increase your spouse's feelings of self-worth. The result is that your spouse's capacity to love and give in return is enhanced.

Elizabeth Barrett Browning described the essence of edifying when she wrote to the man she would marry, "Make thy love larger to enlarge my worth."

To encourage your spouse is to inspire him or her with renewed courage, spirit and hope. It is an act of affirmation for who the person is.

Marriage Involves Intimacy

Marriage is a way of life, a celebration of life. A wedding ends but a marriage progresses until the death of one of the partners. The conclusion of the wedding marks the beginning of a marriage relationship which is a call to intimacy. Intimacy is shared identity, a "we" relationship. Its opposite is a marriage in which the individuals are called "married singles"—each partner goes his own way. In shared intimacy there must be a level of honesty that makes each vulnerable to the other. Intimacy is a multi-stringed musical instrument. The music from a viola comes not from one string but from a combination of different strings and finger positions.

We hear a great deal today about physical intimacy, often referring to nothing more than the physical act of two bodies copulating. However, the basis for true physical intimacy actually results from two other critical areas—*emotional intimacy* and *aesthetic intimacy.*

A physical marriage involves the marriage of emotions as well as bodies. Emotions give color to life. Emotional intimacy eludes many couples because one or both make no conscious effort to develop its potential. A man's and woman's emotions may be at different levels and intensities, or a woman's priority may be emotional intimacy whereas the man's priority is physical. When a couple learns to share the emotional level, when they can understand and experience each other's feelings, they are well on the way to achieving true intimacy. Barriers and walls must be lowered for intimacy to develop.

Judson Swihart writes of the tragedy of a marriage lacking emotional intimacy. "Some people are like medieval castles.

Their high walls keep them safe from being hurt. They protect themselves emotionally by permitting no exchange of feelings with others. No one can enter. They are secure from attack. However, inspection of the occupant finds him or her lonely, rattling around his castle alone. The castle dweller is a self-made prisoner. He or she needs to feel loved by someone, but the walls are so high that it is difficult to reach out or for anyone else to reach in. [8]

Marriage Is a Call to Suffering

The key issue to life's crises is our response. When trouble comes we may say, "God, this isn't what I wanted in my life, I didn't plan for this." But the trouble is there, regardless of our wishes. How will we respond to it?

A verse that has meant so much to me is one I ask couples in premarital counseling to build their marriage upon: "Consider it all joy, my brethren, when you encounter various trials; knowing that the testing [or trying] of your faith produces endurance" (Jas. 1:2-3 *NASB*). It's easy to read a passage like this and say, "Well, that's fine." It is another thing, however, to put it into practice.

What does the word "consider" actually mean? It refers to an internal attitude of the heart or the mind that allows the trial and circumstance of life to affect us adversely or beneficially. Another way James 1:2 might be translated is: "Make up your mind to regard adversity as something to welcome or be glad about."

You have the power to decide what your attitude will be. You can approach it and say: "It's terrible. Totally upsetting. This is the last thing I wanted for my life. Why did it have to happen now? Why me?"

The other way of "considering" the same difficulty is to say: "It's not what I wanted or expected but it's here. There are going to be some difficult times, but how can I make the best of them?" Don't ever deny the pain or the hurt that you might have to go through, but always ask, "What can I learn from it and how can it be used for God's glory?"

The verb tense used in the word consider indicates a decisiveness of action. It's not an attitude of resignation—"Well, I'll just give up. I'm just stuck with this problem. That's the way life is." If you resign yourself, you will sit back and not put forth any effort. The verb tense actually indicates that you will have to go against your natural inclination to see the trial as a negative force. There will be some moments when you won't see it like that at all and then you'll have to remind yourself: "No, I think there is a better way of responding to this. Lord, I really want you to help me see it from a different perspective." And then your mind will shift to a more constructive response. This often takes a lot of work on your part.

God created us with both the capacity and the freedom to determine how we will respond to those unexpected incidents which life brings our way. You may honestly wish that a certain event had never occurred. But you cannot change the fact.

My wife, Joyce, and I have had to learn to look to God in the midst of a seeming tragedy. We have two children; a daughter, Sheryl, who is now 24, and a son, Matthew, who is 18. Mentally, however, Matthew is at less than a two-year-old level. He is a brain-damaged, mentally retarded boy who may never develop past the mental level of a three-year-old. Matthew can walk but he cannot talk or feed himself; he is not toilet trained. He is classified as profoundly retarded.

We did not anticipate becoming the parents of a mentally retarded son. We married upon graduation from college, proceeded through seminary and graduate school training, and into a local church ministry. Several years later, Matthew was born. We have learned and grown through the process of caring for him. As I look at my life I know that I have been an impatient, selfish person in many ways. But because of Matthew I have had the opportunity to develop patience. When you wait a long time for a child to be able to reach out and handle an item, when you wait three or four years for him to learn to walk, you develop patience. We have had to learn to be sensitive to a person who cannot verbally communicate his needs, hurts or wants. We must decipher what he is trying to say; we must try to interpret his nonverbal behavior.

Needless to say, Joyce and I have grown and changed through this process. We have experienced times of hurt, frustration and sorrow. But we have rejoiced and learned to thank God for those tiny steps of progress most people would take completely for granted. The meaning of the name Matthew—"God's gift" or "gift from God"—has become very real to us.

We might very easily have chosen bitterness over our son's problem. We could have let it become a source of estrangement in our marriage, hindering our growth as individuals. But God enabled us to select the path of acceptance. We have grown and matured. Together. Not instantly, but over the course of several years. There have been steep places to overcome. But there have also been highlights and rich moments of reflection and delight. Matthew has become the refining agent that God is using to change us.

My wife and I have discovered a great deal about the way God works. We realize that He prepared us years before for Matthew's coming, though we hadn't realized the preparation was taking place. When I was in seminary I was required to write a thesis. Not knowing what to write about, I asked one of my professors to suggest a topic. She assigned me the title, "The Christian Education of the Mentally Retarded Child." I knew absolutely nothing on the subject, but I learned in a hurry. I read books, went to classes, observed training sessions in hospitals and homes, and finally wrote the thesis. I rewrote it three times and my wife typed it three times before it was accepted.

Later on, my graduate studies in psychology required several hundred hours of internship in a school district. The school district assigned me the task of testing mentally retarded children and placing them in their respective classes.

While serving as minister of education in a church for six years, I was asked by the church board to develop a Sunday School program for retarded children. My duties included developing the ministry and the curriculum, and training the teachers.

Two years before Matthew was born, Joyce and I were talking one evening. One of us said, "Isn't it interesting that we have all this exposure to retarded children? We've been learning so much. Could it be that God is preparing us for something that is going to occur later on in our life?" That's all we said at the time and I can't even remember which one of us said it. Within a year, Matthew was born. Eight months later his seizures began. The uncertainty we had felt over the rate of his progress was now a deep concern. When we learned the full truth we began to see how the Lord had prepared us.

Where does the call to suffering enter this whole process? Romans 8:16-17 *(NASB)* says, "The Spirit Himself bears witness with our spirit that we are children of God, and if children, heirs also, heirs of God and fellow-heirs with Christ, if indeed we suffer with Him in order that we may also be glorified with Him." As members of the Body of Christ, we suffer when one member suffers.

In the minor or major crises which will occur in your marriage, each partner will experience hurt. Hurt shared, diminishes; carried alone it expands. Lewis B. Smedes describes marital suffering in this way:

> Anybody's marriage is a harvest of suffering. Romantic lotus-eaters may tell you marriage was designed to be a pleasure-dome for erotic spirits to frolic in self-fulfilling relations. But they play you false. Your marriage vow was a promise to suffer. Yes, to suffer; I will not take it back. You promised to suffer with. It made sense, because the person you married was likely to get hurt along the route, sooner or later, more or less, but hurt. And you promised to hurt with your spouse. A marriage is a life of shared pain.[9]

This is a privilege! This is our ministry to one another! This is a reflection of the gift of marriage! How will you respond to this aspect of marriage?[10]

As you read on in this book two vital topics are not covered for lack of space. They are the sexual relationship and finances, and both areas can hinder your marriage relationship. For complete information I would recommend the tape series "Before the Wedding Night" by Dr. Ed Wheat and "Your Finances in Changing Times" by Larry Burkett. Both are available from Christian Marriage Enrichment, 1913 E. 17th Street #118, Santa Ana, CA 92701.

2
COMMITMENT TO BE FREE FROM THE PAST

You're about to be married and you are looking forward to a life of satisfaction and love in this new relationship. You want your marriage to be everything you dream about and so do I. But there is one significant barrier that could stand in the way of happiness in your marriage. Do you have any idea what it might be? It's this: unresolved issues from your past that are still affecting and influencing your life. Oh, I know, we are all products of our past in one way or another. What I'm talking about is the kind of experiences or relationships from your past that keep your life from going forward or that continue to direct how you react and respond to your fiancé. I'm sure you want to be an independent person, free from negative influences from the past. But are you really?

In America the creed of independence is so strong we often feel a need to achieve our own individual independence. "I am my own person; I have risen above my life experiences and my past." It sounds good, but most of us are not nearly as independent and free as we would like to believe we are.

For many of us, unresolved relationships and issues of the past are still guiding our lives and hampering communication. Some of us even suffer because of a half-resolved and half-buried past. Because we react and respond to others on the basis of unresolved past relationships, we actually perpetuate those difficulties.

Some of us carry wounds from the past, some carry scars. Some of us have buried our painful memories, hoping those memories never resurrect.

As we grow older our storehouse of memories increases. Our personalities and general makeup are the results of those memories. Many of our feelings of joy, hurt, anger or delight are tied into how we remember events and experiences.

You and I will remember the same event in a very different way. For example, I may remember the enjoyment and delight of a day in the mountains hiking to a lake. You may remember the 10-hour drive, arising at 4:00 A.M. and feeling exhausted for three days. We both experienced the same events but different aspects made an impression.

Much of the suffering in marriages today is caused by memories. The forgotten anniversary, a bitter fight, the discovery of an affair and numerous other events continue to fester and simmer in our minds. Sometimes we try to hide these memories in the recesses of our minds. A usual response to an undesirable memory is to repress or forget it. Who wants to remember the pains of the past? Let's live as though they did not occur.

Hiding unpleasant memories, however, prevents them from being completely healed. Thus they continue to act as an anchor which we drag along with us as we limp through life. When we bury memories and wounds we bury them alive. And their resurrection comes when we least suspect it. Painful memories must be dredged up and faced for healing to occur.

Buried memories surface anew when we encounter problems in our marriage, and the past may determine how we deal with those problems. Some marry hoping that the marriage will serve as a blotter to eradicate the past. They soon learn, however, that the past sticks with them. Marriage does not change our past—it works in just the opposite way. Marriage can reveal past hurts and all our efforts to keep those memories hidden may eventually result in a crumbling marriage.

Where Memories Begin

Where do our memories begin? How might they influence

you and your attempts to communicate with your fiancé?

What is the earliest memory you can recall? One of my earliest memories is a series of images which come to mind when I think of a trip I took with my parents across the United States at the age of four.

What are the five earliest memories you can recall?

What is the earliest positive memory you can recall? One that comes to my mind was a fishing trip at a creek with my brother and cousin. We pulled in fish after fish and it was a delightful experience.

What is the earliest painful memory you can recall? A painful memory for me was a spanking I got with a switch because I had misbehaved.

The Inner Child of the Past

Childhood memories are more than remembrances. Feelings and attitudes from even the earliest of years can determine your present-day responses. Some can enable you to move forward in your life. Others interfere. Bottled-up unpleasant memories conflict with your adult life. Dr. Hugh Missildine describes these memories as the "inner child of the past." This child still seeks to control your life. Part of your discomfort arises because many of the feelings are not unreasonable for a child, but seem undesirable and unreasonable for an adult.

There are times when you ask, "Why do I *say* what I do?" "Why do I *act* the way I do?" "What is wrong with me?" "Why do I feel this way?" You may become angry at yourself for these feelings. You may even criticize yourself for these inner feelings. But attempts to deny or repress them only create a greater discomfort. Because you don't share this struggle with others, the difficulty is compounded.

Many of your memories fall into the category of unresolved childhood conflict—your "child of the past." Who usually responds to you as a child? Your parents. But what do you do when you're an adult and your parents are not around or are dead? Who parents your "child" then? You do. Whether you realize it or not, you have assumed the attitudes and beliefs of your parents so that you respond to yourself and to others the way they did, even though these attitudes are not your own. Thus your communication is not really your own. You respond to life partly as a mature adult and partly as your child of the past.

The Old Patterns of the Past

In becoming your own parent you cling to old patterns from the past because they are familiar. And you give in to them even though they hurt, because to live in the unfamiliar present means breaking free of the familiar. And it takes effort to break away from the past.

Your past emerges more clearly when you marry. Dr. Hugh Missildine has suggested that marriage involves four people and not *two*! There are two adults who act in the present and the two children who respond because of their family background and memories. This certainly complicates a marriage, to say the least! Without realizing it you carry into marriage hidden aspects of your childhood nature. We all do this even though we have heard the admonition from Scripture again and again: "When I was a child, I talked like a child, I thought like a child, I reasoned like a child; now that I have become a man, I am done with childish ways and have put them aside" (1 Cor. 13:11, *AMP*).

During the courtship we try to emphasize our mature adult qualities to impress the other. But once we are married we relax. We make our new home into a place of comfort and soon feel familiar in our surroundings. Now it becomes an atmosphere wherein we can allow patterns from the past to emerge. Haven't you heard husbands and wives say, "He wasn't like this before we married"? Or, "I never saw this side of her before"?

A wife's memory may be of a home that was a show place. She remembers her mother telling her for years that a good wife keeps an impeccable home. So she never allows her home to be messy. She wants to be a good wife doesn't she? Her husband, however, sees home as a place of cluttered refuge where neatness and order do not exist! Why? He too has messages and images from the past and perhaps he is following the example set by his own father. Many of us consciously or unconsciously attempt to duplicate the familiar patterns of our childhood.

The child in us had numerous expectations. How we communicated in our childhood home will be brought into our marriage. In many cases the difference in communication patterns and styles between husband and wife is as complicated as two foreign nations getting together. Dr. Missildine takes this point a step further:

> Generally, in order to achieve the "at home" feeling within our marriage, we treat ourselves in the same way our parents treated us. The old "at home" emotional atmosphere of childhood is copied as precisely as possible, including any painful attitudes that may have characterized our family life in the past. We frequently even invite our spouse to treat us the way our parents did—unknowingly seeking their approval and depending on their evaluation of us in the same way that we once sought the approval and love of our parents. This is, in a way, what is happening when your spouse refuses, perhaps by default or abdication, to assume responsibility or "acts like a baby."[1]

If we could realize that each of us has both an adult part and a child part within us which is (hopefully) still in a growth stage, we may become a bit more accepting of one another.

From our earliest days we feel a sense of attachment to our parents. They supply our wants and needs, including a sense of stability. In the same way that we rely on them, we come to rely on childhood patterns that persist far into adulthood. We may feel very conscious of this and feel immobilized in trying to deal with it, or it could seem a phantom, illusive attachment that still maintains control over our responses. Either way, childhood patterns, whether healthy or painful, are familiar, and familiarity brings security and comfort.

For example, our attraction and attachment to particular people in adulthood can be a carry-over from our past. If our parents were loving, they were bound to leave their stamp upon our lives, even if we cannot remember the specifics of that relationship. Some of us, in our adulthood, are drawn to people who are like our parents in many ways. Others are drawn to those people opposite from their parents.

An example of this kind of attachment is a woman named Mary. As she dated she seemed to be drawn to men who were not really good for her. She realized that she was drawn to men with some type of flaw. Her own father was a very handsome but passive and ineffective man. From early childhood she greatly admired him and struggled not to see his weaknesses. But after so many years of disappointment, she felt betrayed. Nevertheless, she still chose to date men who were like her father, hoping that they would turn out to be dependable and that she might be able to help them.

John's experience reflects another variation of this tendency. He was raised by a mother who was cold, aloof and unresponsive. She was extremely neat and was more concerned with her home being a show place than in nurturing the members of her family. She dressed well and did not want her son to get too close because he might "mess up her clothes or hair." He felt she used him because she always told him what to do, how to do it and what to wear—especially when she entertained. Although John was raised without warmth, love and nurturing, who does he date again and again? Women who cannot give of themselves and who are little more than unloving mannequins. Why? He keeps trying to refashion women like his mother, in order to make them give him what he needed. He selects women with little potential to give him what he needs and becomes frustrated in his attempts to reform them.

This attachment in dating often continues into mate selection. Some people try to recreate their original family. For example, an only child who has not had much experience relating to his own peer group is more likely to select a parent figure for a spouse. Some people select for a mate a person who is some type of transference object from their past—someone who is like a parent, sibling or other significant person to whom they can respond and relate as they did the person from their past. Most of us do this to some degree. But if there are unresolved emotional issues still existing between us and that significant person from the past, there can be problems. For example, you might choose a partner who is similar to someone you could not get along with in your past. You cannot get along with this type of person in your present situation either. But you are not always aware that you are repeating your old pattern.

All people do not try to recreate their original families when they marry. Many want just the opposite and look for a spouse who is very different. They are trying to escape from their original family and to build some type of new one. They believe they will be more comfortable with this new type of person. But often in their blindness they may overlook buried similarities that emerge later on. When they do discover these in their mates, they may be thrown into a panic, for it appears their history is about to repeat itself. The greater the amount of unresolved issues from their past family situation, the greater the upset.

Why, you may ask, do people turn so much of their lives over to the influence of significant individuals from their past? Would you believe that we really have no choice in the matter? Why not? Because you began your interaction with your parents in a helpless state. You were dependent upon them for your very existence; you learned this very soon. You also learned that there were certain ways you had to respond to maintain a state of well-being with them. If mother and father were happy, then you received more positive attention. Over the years children develop quite a repertoire of responses to maintain a good relationship.

As you grew, your physical survival depended less and less upon your parents. But your dependence on your parents for good feelings decreases much more slowly. And for some, the decrease is negligible. Dr. Howard Halpern put it so well: "The emotional umbilical cord not only remains uncut but often twists into a Gordian knot that ties us to our parents' reactions to us."[2]

Evaluating the Past

Let's take some time now to evaluate your past. Be sure to answer each question. Perhaps you would like to write your responses on a piece of paper. Then share your responses with your fiancé.

1. Evaluate your life by completing your own family history.

   a. List what you feel are/were the positive qualities of your father.

   b. List what you feel are/were the negative qualities of your father.

   c. Describe how you feel/felt about your father.

   d. What emotions does/did he express openly to you and how?

   e. Describe how you and your father communicate/communicated.

   f. Describe the most pleasant and unpleasant experiences with your father.

g. What messages did your father give you about yourself? Were they positive or negative? Please describe.

h. Describe how your father punished or criticized you.

i. In what ways are you different from your father?

j. List what you feel are/were the positive qualities of your mother.

k. List what you feel are/were the negative qualities of your mother.

l. Describe how you feel/felt about your mother.

m. What emotions does/did she express openly and how?

n. Describe how you and your mother communicate/communicated.

o. Describe the most pleasant and unpleasant experiences with your mother.

p. What messages did your mother give you about yourself? Were they positive or negative? Please describe.

q. Describe how your mother punished or criticized you.

r. In what ways are you different from your mother?

2. Using a line graph, describe the history of your personal relationship with your father from infancy to the present time.

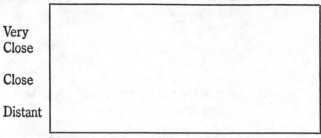

Very
Close

Close

Distant

　　　Birth-5　5-10　10-15　15-20　20-present time

a. What made the relationship close?

b. What made the relationship distant?

3. Use a line graph to describe the history of your personal relationship with your mother from infancy to the present time.

Very
Close

Close

Distant

　　　Birth-5　5-10　10-15　15-20　20-present time

a. What made the relationship close?

b. What made the relationship distant?

4. Graph the history with the sibling of the opposite sex who is closest in age to you. (Use the same sex if necessary.)

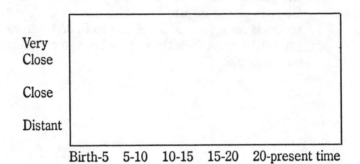

Very
Close

Close

Distant

Birth-5   5-10   10-15   15-20   20-present time

5. Describe the relationship your parents had as you grew up. Did they openly express feelings? Did they ever argue or fight? Was one domineering? Describe the kinds of difficulties you sensed between your parents. How did you feel about their relationship?

6. What were you most afraid of as a child (criticism, failure, rejection, competition, darkness, getting injured)? Tell, as best you can, about the circumstances when you were most likely to have this fear.

7. Did you have any Christian training? Describe the role God has played in your life. What concerns, fears or problems have you had in relation to God? When were you first aware of them? What have been your most serious concerns?

8. List 10 adjectives that describe you.

1. _____   6. _____

2. _____   7. _____

3. _____   8. _____

4. _____   9. _____

5. _____   10. _____

Which of these adjectives are characteristic of each of the following?

Spouse _____

Father _____

Mother _____

Brother _____

Sister _____

Friend _____

9. Where on the following line would you place yourself currently in relationship to your parents?

completely   completely
dependent   independent

10. Write out your earliest memory.

Patterns from the Past

One of our tasks as adults is to identify our thoughts and feelings and discover their origin. Recognizing them may be the easiest task, accepting or modifying them may be difficult. Many of these memories (thoughts and feelings) are the basis for how we feel about ourselves. Many of us carry around distorted views of ourselves. These too stem from childhood and are continuations of our past that may have been created by longtime parental attitudes. But blaming our parents for who and what we are today has no value. All parents are fallible, we all make mistakes. Most parents do the best they can. We are now responsible for how we continue to treat ourselves.

What types of experiences may affect you even now from your childhood? If you came from a home where you were overcoerced, you either are very submissive or you have learned to passively resist other's suggestions. You were not taught to be independent because your parents gave you constant direction, supervision, redirections, instructions and reminders.

If your parents were overly submissive to your own demands, your present life may be characterized by impulsive behavior. You experience excesses in your life, you may be thoughtless, are easily angered and do not consider the rights of others.

If your parents were punitive or neglectful, you may have feelings of hatred or animosity. You may have learned to behave in such a way to reinforce or justify your parents' response. You may have developed the belief that you deserve punishment. If you were neglected, you may find it difficult to develop close meaningful relationships with others or to develop a self-identity that helps you relate to others.

Let's consider two other patterns from your past in more detail.

The Effects of Personal Rejection

What happened if you experienced a great deal of rejection as a child or adolescent? Many people grow up from childhood with the belief that acceptance and affection have a price tag— they are not free gifts, but something one earns by accomplishing something, attaining some goal or refraining from doing something.

During his childhood one man I counseled never felt free to make any noise or disruption at home. Noise was absolutely forbidden. When friends came over to see him, he would become embarrassed if they were loud or noisy in front of his parents. Today, as an adult, he rarely experiences any peace or feels relaxed. He is constantly edgy. Because of his parents' restriction against noise, he interpreted this to mean that they did not appreciate him. He also remembers feeling that he was never "good" enough. Even though he may not have actually been rejected by his parents, he felt that he was.

Rejection communicates to you that you are not worth having a relationship with or even knowing. If rejection occurs to any degree, you feel hurt and even bitter. The hurt remains with you and you become very sensitive to actual or apparent rebuffs. You tend to anticipate rejection and read it into other people's responses. You assume the worst to begin with and are very suspicious. It is difficult to be open with some people, for show-ing true feelings may lead to another painful rejection.

You also tend to reject yourself if you feel you were rejected by someone you cared for. You treat yourself like a criminal and end up directing more criticism and disapproval toward yourself than your parents or others ever gave you. Do you cheer your-self on in life or do you make disapproving and rejecting com-ments to yourself? Are you a worse critic than others? Do you ever say, "You're too sensitive"; "You won't succeed"; "You're not worth loving"? You may be rejecting yourself if you do. How do you parent yourself?

Part of your inner struggle, however, may focus around some unanswered questions. You may feel guilty or somehow responsible for your parents' rejection of you. And, if so, you may have feelings of worthlessness that contribute to your con-tinuing suspiciousness. What then could others see in you? Why would they want to be involved with you? And if this is so, you may have developed a protective armor, like a porcupine, to ward off involvement with other people.

If you received rejection as a child, rather than love, you may have felt puzzled. You saw other parents giving their child love and acceptance. Why were you not receiving love, too?

If you are a rejected person, you may enter marriage starved for love and acceptance. If you marry a rejected person, you marry a starving person. If you both were rejected, watch out! Your expectations and demands on one another will lead you to heights of frustration, anger and disappointment.

Once in a married relationship, the rejected person's need for attention, acceptance and affection is constant. This puts a great burden on the partner. When the spouse is unable to respond at times with the same intensity of affection the rejected person expects, the person feels rejected again. He/she may then become depressed, angry or hurt and make even more demands on his/her mate for love and acceptance.

If a rejected person constantly questions his/her partner's love for him/her, trouble is on the horizon. After awhile the part-ner will become fed up with being doubted and say, "You can believe what you want to believe. Either you take what I say at face value or you don't. I don't have any other way of convincing you and I am sick and tired of trying. I give up!" Of course, this will just create more seeming rejection, even though the partner's frustration is certainly justified. People do not like to have their word doubted or to have their love constantly tested. When such a situation continues for a long period of time, the partner becomes angry. No matter what he/she does, it is not enough.

Some rejected people actually seek out a marriage partner who will repeat what they experienced as a child. They are familiar and comfortable with the same kind of distance and mistreatment they experienced for so many years. Then if the rejecter-type partner never shows approval or acceptance, the rejected one relives his/her old familiar pattern. The rejected partner doesn't realize that he/she will never gain acceptance from someone who, because of his/her own inadequacies and deficiencies, has little or nothing to give. It is like going to a dry well for water.

Some of us tend to be perfectionists. A perfectionist probably received parental messages which included: "You can do better"; "That's not good enough"; "Always do better than others"; "You'll receive love if you perform"; "Beat the next guy." We remember comments, words, withheld praise, double messages, sad faces, frowns, signs of disappointment, requests for more this, more that, etc. And thus the treadmill of striving is perpetuated.

The perfectionist has an endless goal of pleasing his parents. Even though the parents may no longer be around, their parental message is still a recurring childhood memory. This colors the perfectionist's inner conversations and how he responds outwardly. Those around him must also perform: "If I must be perfect, so must they. I must urge them on, criticize, correct, make them perfect as I must be perfect. Never let up on them. Everyone can do better." What happens when others slack off and are not perfect? The perfectionist becomes anxious because the lack of perfect behavior in others arouses his own feelings of self-belittlement. His feeling is that no one ever succeeds, including himself. His striving is a desire to escape this constant feeling of "I could have done better."

A perfectionist is difficult to live with. If you are this individual, let me illustrate what you probably do. You are demanding of yourself and possibly of your fiancé. You exert tremendous energy to accomplish an ever-elusive goal. Everything must be in its place; colors must match; every item has to be properly lined up on the table; you must say the right phrase; be punctual; etc. You may give great attention to every little detail and become upset when you cannot regulate all of your life or the life of your partner. The problem is you are never satisfied with your own or with your fiancé's performance.

You experience success but still feel empty and dissatisfied. You may feel like a "successful failure." Many of us are successful and proficient and can rest in what we have accomplished, feeling good about our attainment. Often what we do benefits and serves others. We are satisfied. The perfectionist, however, strives for his own benefit and does not find satisfaction. His cry is, "I must do better, better, better!"

In relationships, the message is, "I could have done better." There is always the elusive promise of future acceptance if only a better job is done. But it never really occurs. The perfectionist's communication patterns reflect his feelings. By continuing to use the same belittling expressions and statements he undermines himself and his relationships.

We do not need a list of achievements to prove ourselves as persons of worth. When we think of our worth as an achievement rather than a gift, we end up on a treadmill. We need not fear losing our worth, because God's estimation of us is not based upon our qualifications. He created us in His image as persons of value and worth. If we feel our worth has to be achieved, then we must be constantly concerned about any threat to our performance.

The perfectionist's fear of failure is a fear of the sense of worthlessness. He has learned to focus more on what he lacks than on what he has. But when we can believe that our worth is a gift from God, we are free to risk because worth remains stable whether we achieve or not. We are free to attempt new ventures which could actually enhance this gift of worth. God's act in our life is an emancipation. We are free from the infringement of fearful hesitation and perfectionistic striving.

The Effects of Indulgence

Some of us came from yet a different home environment which affects our life and our marriage. Our parents may have thought that the best way to express their love to us was through indulgence. As a child we were given, given, given! Even before we asked, we received. Even if there was no interest or need on our part, material items, attention and services were provided. A child in this type of home atmosphere has little opportunity to learn satisfaction from his own efforts. The child is almost kept in a dependent passive state and does not learn to take initiative. Instead, he learns to expect others to provide for him and entertain him. You would probably label this person selfish or self-centered.

What kind of messages does this child receive? He believes that others will and should provide for him. He doesn't have to do much to receive attention, affection, gifts, etc. He demands whatever he wants and feels little need to provide anything in return. He is generally passive with high expectations of others. How will these childhood messages and memories affect marriage? Watch and see.

An overindulged partner expects his/her spouse to be a mind reader and when the spouse isn't, he/she complains—not always outwardly but in inner conversations. He/she feels frustrated, annoyed, restless and hurt. When the complaints do come they may sound like this:

"My wife ought to know I like . . . "

"My wife should know how I'm feeling . . . "

"My husband ought to do most of the housework for me so I can go out."

"Why should I tell him? If he truly loves me he should know what I want."

This person is a taker and not a giver. Intimacy and emotional involvement in marriage cannot develop. He has no concern over disappointing his partner. He resists any efforts on the part of his partner to help him become a contributing member of the marriage. He will find many ways to escape giving.

These are just brief illustrations of how your childhood may still be with you. There are many other ways in which these patterns emerge.

How can the influence of your memories be changed? How can your childhood messages be altered?

Blaming your circumstances or your parents is not the solution. Your parents were human and fallible. You may feel resentment, anger and bitterness toward them because of what they either did or did not do. But in making them your scapegoat you simply rid yourself of the responsibility for the way you are today. You *can* do something about the *continuation* of parental attitudes and memories that continue to influence you. For these you *are* responsible. Perhaps if you become a better parent to yourself you can become a more mature child to your parents.

Let me ask you two important questions: In what way is the presence of Jesus Christ in your life disconnecting your responses from your past to the present? Are you becoming a free person who is living your present life without heavy anchors from the past slowing you down?

Perhaps you have not yet applied Jesus Christ to your life in this area. You can ask Him to free the bondage from your mind so you will have greater understanding and awareness of your past experiences. You can ask Him for clarity of thought in accurately recalling those memories. Ask Him to help you identify how you continue to treat yourself as others treated you in early years.

May I make some specific but strong suggestions? Please do not marry without first becoming fully aware of any issues from the past that might interfere with your marriage. And then, please take the steps necessary to free yourself from any past bondage so your marriage relationship has a chance.

This chapter was written to help you become aware of this area and identify issues, not to resolve them. The resolution of these past issues can occur. Here are three specific suggestions to help you get started:

1. Read my book *Making Peace with Your Past,* published by Fleming H. Revell. This book is available at Christian book-

stores or from Christian Marriage Enrichment.

2. Listen to the series of tapes by Dr. David Seamands entitled *Biblical Psychology*. These tapes include the topics: "Damaged Emotions," "The Healing of Memories," "The Hidden Child in Us All," "Hidden Tormentors," and others.

These tapes are also available from Christian Marriage Enrichment, 1913 E. 17th St., #118, Santa Ana, CA 92701.

3. If necessary, seek out a qualified Christian counselor to help you work through these issues. Marriage can be hard enough without unnecessary burdens from the past.

Remember that Jesus Christ came to set us free—free from the consequences of sin and death, but also free from the crippling patterns and experiences of the past.

3
COMMITMENT TO LOVE

The couple sat in my office during their first session of pre-marital counseling. We were coming to the place where we would be talking about three very important issues for their marriage. They had been given the questions in advance in order to thoughtfully think and pray about their answers. The questions were:

1. Why is this the time of your life to marry?
2. List 10 or 12 specific reasons why you want to marry this person.
3. Describe why you love your fiancé and describe the type of love you have for this person.

Before we proceed, if you were the couple seated in my office, how would you respond to those questions? Take some time right now to consider your responses before reading any further.

These questions can help you clarify how solid your foundation is for this important step of marriage. It is better to clarify and define your responses now than to wonder a few years hence, "Why did I marry?" or "Was that the right time in my life to marry?"

Why Marry Now?

It is important to clarify that this really is the time in your life to marry. Often a person's emotions and passions run ahead of his or her reason and the will of God. As you read earlier, people do marry for a mixture of reasons. It is important for both you and your fiancé to be clearly aware of those reasons. I have found with many couples that after having listed their reasons for marriage, they incorporate their answers into their wedding ceremony in order to let other people know why they are marrying.

Here is one young man's list of reasons why he should marry now. I left them exactly as he wrote them and shared them with his fiancé and me during our session together:

Eight Indications Why This Is the Time to Marry

1. I now have enough experience living alone to know that I prefer not to.
2. I now know that I am able to financially support a wife.
3. However, I expect to be much more secure financially in the relatively near future and I want to get married before then because I think it can be beneficial to a good relationship to share some minor economic deprivations in the beginning.
4. I may be making my final career decision in the near future and I would like my wife to be able to share in that decision.
5. I want to leave the Riverside, California area as soon as practical and I want to be able to take Mary with me.
6. If I am going to have children I don't want to wait much longer to start having them.
7. I want to go to Europe with my wife while we are both still young enough to enjoy doing it on a very limited budget.
8. But mainly, having made the major decision that getting married will greatly improve my life, I am just naturally eager to start enjoying that improved lifestyle as soon as possible.

Why Marry This Particular Person?

I remember working one time with a young man who was a lawyer. He was very thoughtful and insightful as he reflected on why he wanted to marry his fiancé. Think about what he is saying in his list:

The Twelve Reasons Why I'm Marrying Betty:

1. The Lord is first in her life. It happened last January because she was tired of calling her own shots. Consistently has followed that up with a desire to learn, prayer, fellowship and witnessing.
2. Little girl nature—modest dress, looks young, spontaneity, loves cows and cute things.
3. Reaches out to other people—senses needs and puts love into action, not just on a one-time basis, but consistent follow-up. Example—neighbors, friends and work.
4. Responsibility and common sense—Boss said that seldom has he seen a more dedicated person and one with so much skill in speech therapy. I trust her with maps and directions, to sometimes handle arrangements when I'm not able. Sets goals and meets them, a budget.
5. She laughs with joy in her heart—she loves pure things, clean and crisp. She doesn't complain a lot, is willing to roll with the punches. She loves life and wants to reach out and grab it.
6. She cries—she has a depth of feeling for many different situations, work, person who is lost. She uses it to accept her womanhood.
7. She's devoted to our relationship—she's uplifting, encouraging. She speaks the truth in love. She cares what I feel and respects my desires and interests. She desires to work hard at making it work. She's affectionate and warm.

8. She's intelligent—similar educational background.
9. She sees our relationship as a team ministry. We're walking in the same direction with a common goal, to spread the teaching and life of our Lord Jesus.
10. She's cute (size, shape, face, hair) and clean (neat in appearance, takes care of herself).
11. She's a quick learner. When new things come her way she desires to incorporate them into her life and moves on to the next step.
12. She loves fires, daisies and poems, i.e., very romantic, loves beauty and purity. Enjoys relaxing with the simple things.

Not everyone is that articulate. Most people list their reasons in short, simple statements—which is perfectly all right.

Sometimes as people share their reasons some surprises occur. I remember an occasion when a young lady was listening to her fiancé's reasons for marrying her. The more he read the angrier she became and before he completed the reasons, she broke in and said, "The reason you want to marry me is for me to do everything for you! What are you going to do for me? Don't you really love me?" The rest of the session was spent talking about the reasons and motivations for their marriage. We were able to settle some of the differences right then and there.

Why Do You Love Your Fiancé?

The last question we cover concerns love—what it is and why you love the other person. It is so important to be clear about this. I would like you to think carefully about the emotion, the passion, the commitment of love which is a clear act of the will.

Every person needs to receive love and to give love. That is one of the reasons you are choosing to marry. These two needs are basic for all people. We demonstrate our inner feelings of love through our behavior. Some of our behaviors are loving and some are not. The Scriptures, speaking directly about behaviors, say that we are to "put on" loving behaviors and "put off"

non-loving behaviors: "Lay aside every weight, and the sin"
(see Heb. 12:1-2, *KJV*). Look up some of the Scripture refer-
ences in the following list.

Put Off	Scriptural Insights	Put On
1. Lack of Love	1 John 4:7-8,20 John 15:12	Love
2. Judging	Matthew 7:1-2 John 8:9; 15:22	Self-Examination
3. Bitterness	Hebrews 12:15 Colossians 3:12	Tenderhearted
4. Unforgiving Spirit	Mark 11:25 Matthew 6:14	Forgiving Spirit
5. Pride	Proverbs 16:18 James 4:6	Humility
6. Boasting (conceit)	1 Corinthians 4:7 Proverbs 27:2	Humility
7. Hatred	Matthew 5:21-22 1 Corinthians 13:3	Love or Kindness
8. Gossip	1 Timothy 5:13 1 Peter 2:9	Speaking with praise
9. Lying	Ephesians 4:25 Zechariah 8:16	Speaking Truth
10. Profanity	Psalm 109:17 1 Timothy 4:12	Edification
11. Idle Words	Matthew 12:36 Proverbs 21:23	Bridle the Tongue

12. Ingratitude	Romans 1:21 Ephesians 5:20	Thankfulness
13. Impatience	James 1:2-4 Hebrews 10:36	Patience
14. Murmuring	Proverbs 19:3 1 Thessa- lonians 5:18	Gratefulness
15. Complaining	Jude 15–16 Hebrews 13:5	Contentment
16. Irritation to others	Proverbs 25:8 Philippians 2:3-4	Preferring in love
17. Jealousy	Proverbs 27:4 1 Corin- thians 13:7	Trust, preferring others
18. Strife	James 3:16 Luke 6:31	Esteem of others
19. Losing temper	Proverbs 16:32 Romans 5:3-4	Self-Control
20. Complacency	James 4:17 Colossians 3:23	Diligence

We say that we marry for love, but what type of love? Let's look at three different types of love and their effects upon marriage.

Love in Three Forms

Eros

Eros is need love. It is the love that leads to marriage. Most couples begin their marriage with a preponderance of eros love and a minimum of the others. Eros is necessary for marriage to succeed. Often it begins in attraction (see diagram 1).

Eros is the love that seeks sensual expression. Eros is

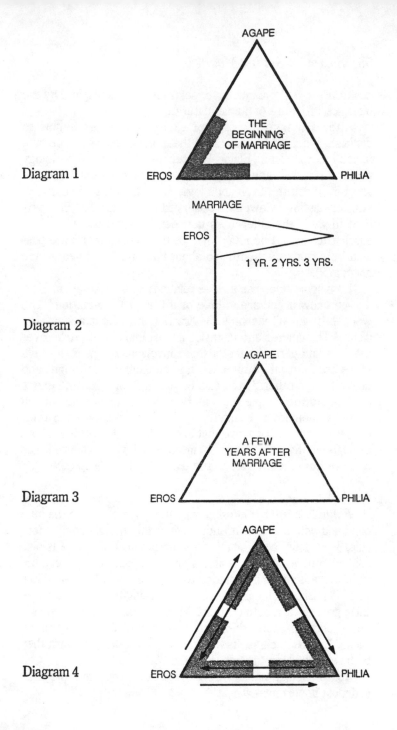

Diagram 1

Diagram 2

Diagram 3

Diagram 4

desire. Eros is a romantic love, sexual love. It is inspired by the biological structure of human nature.

After marriage the eros or excitement phase begins to diminish. We need to remember that a marriage cannot be sustained by eros alone. Elaine Walster, psychology and sociology professor at the University of Wisconsin, has confirmed the short-lived nature of romantic love. Over the past 15 years Dr. Walster has interviewed or observed more than 100,000 persons to study the differences between "passionate" and "compassionate" love. She found that for most couples, intense passion lasts from six months to about two-and-a-half years (see diagram 2).

Eros sometimes has a close relationship to infatuation. How do you know if you are in love or if it is just infatuation? The word "infatuation" means to be "carried away by irrational passions." The desires and fantasies almost immediately take over the lives and personalities of those involved. It's as if all of life stops around that couple. Each is consumed in thought and desire for the other. Often this occurs in a romantic and exotic setting and the couple feels as though they are being carried away by their love. Everything else is dismissed from their minds. But this is not a love that endures. This love comes about through emotions and circumstances. For love to endure it has to move from the eros stage to the level of friendship (*philia*).

Philia

Philia love is the friendship love. In a good marriage the husband and wife are also friends. Friendship means companionship. Friendship also means communication. Philia love is also cooperation. While eros is almost always a face-to-face relationship, philia is often a shoulder-to-shoulder relationship. When there is philia, husband and wife are working together on something greater than both of them. They are finding their oneness, not directly in each other, but in their interest in a common cause. In eros each seeks fulfillment in the other; in philia they both seek fulfillment in one mutual goal.

Your marriage needs three loves: eros, philia and the third and most important—*agape*.

Agape

Agape is self-giving love, gift love, the love that goes on loving even when the other person becomes unlovable. Agape can keep erotic love alive or rekindle erotic love that has been lost. Agape love is not just something that happens to you; it's something you make happen. Love is a personal act of commitment. Christ's love (and hence the pattern for our love) is gift love. Christ's love for us is unconditional. Christ's love is eternal love.

Rick Yohn, in *Beyond Spiritual Gifts,* describes how the ancient Greeks used the term agape:

> [Agape] included the emotions but wasn't limited by them. It included a natural affection, but even when it wasn't natural to love, agape loved anyway. This love provided an excellent basis for companionship, but it transcended that phase if the companion failed to love in return.
>
> When the Bible states that God is love, it uses agape. John wrote, "God so loved [agape] the world, that He gave His only begotten Son" (John 3:16). Agape gives. Agape sacrifices. Agape initiates love. "We love, because He first loved us" (1 John 4:19).
>
> Agape loves whether or not the object deserves that love. "But God demonstrates His own love toward us, in that while we were yet sinners, Christ died for us" (Rom. 5:8).
>
> A husband who loves his wife as Christ loved [agape] the church will make every sacrifice to meet her needs (not necessarily all her wants). He will provide for her physical needs of sexual love, financial security, clothes, food, etc. He will provide for her emotional needs like security, affection, understanding, acceptance, the feeling of being wanted, and of feeling necessary to complete him. He will provide for her spiritual needs by encouraging her to grow in the Lord. He will set the example of what it means to walk in the Spirit.[1]

Agape is kindness. It is being sympathetic, thoughtful and sensitive to the needs of your loved one.

In many marriages agape and philia remain at a low level and eros recedes. The passion and excitement that were the mortar holding the marriage together initially are no longer there (see diagram 3). At this point many couples begin to question, "Why am I married? Was I ever in love in the first place?"

But this need not be the pattern for Christian marriages. If individuals would put forth effort to purposely increase philia and agape love, all three types of love would increase (see diagram 4). The friendship love of philia can enhance and enrich both of the others. Both agape and philia can enrich the eros love so it does not have to diminish as much as it usually does. It too can flourish if properly nurtured; and as it does, the other types of love are reinforced. But all three must be given conscious effort.

Agape can keep the marriage going when eros and philia are low. Most people indicate they did *not* fall in love but their love grew over a period of time. You meet someone who is attractive and/or interesting. Then you want to know more about the person. In time feelings begin to develop and then blossom. But equating falling in love with a heart seizure is a rare experience. If love is not given an opportunity to grow and the relationship is hurried into marriage, the divorce probability is very high. Statistics show that those who know each other well before they marry have the greatest probability of making their marriage work.

Here is something to consider before you give your love to that other person. Can you be happy with this person if he or she never changes? Are you loving the person you have now or an imaginary dream? And can you be happy with this person if he or she changes in ways you never dreamed of? A love with its roots in commitment will last through the pressures and pain of life's disappointments.

Think about this.

Love means to commit yourself without guarantee, to give yourself completely in the hope that your love will produce love in the loved person. Love is an act of faith, and whoever is of little faith is also of little love. The perfect love would be one that gives all and expects nothing. It would, of course, be willing and delighted to take anything it was offered, the more the better. But it would ask for nothing. For if one expects nothing and asks nothing, he can never be deceived or disappointed. It is only when love demands that it brings on pain.[2]

Self-Giving Love

Since agape love is the heart of the marital love relationship, let's think some more about this gift of love.

Agape love is a healing force. To demonstrate the power of this love, let's apply it to a critical area that affects marriage—irritability. Irritability is a barrier and it keeps others at a distance if they know it is present within us. It is the launching pad for attack, lashing out, anger, sharp words, resentment and refusal of others' offers to love us.

Agape love is unique in that it causes us to seek to meet the needs of our mate rather than demanding that our own needs be reciprocated. Our irritability and frustration diminish because we are seeking to fulfill another rather than pursuing and demanding our own need satisfaction.

Lewis B. Smedes, in his excellent work *Love Within Limits,* describes the effect of agape love: "Agape love reduces irritability because this love meets our deepest need. As God reaches down to us with His immense gift of eternal life we experience this agape love coming from Him."[3] This act enables us to move toward others with love.

We read in 1 John 4:7,9,14-16,19 *(NASB)*:

Beloved, let us love one another, for love is from God; and every one who loves is born of God and knows God . . . . By this the love of God was manifested in us, that God has sent His only begotten Son into the world so that we might live through Him . . . . And we have

beheld and bear witness that the Father has sent the
Son to be the Savior of the world. Whoever confesses
that Jesus is the Son of God, God abides in him, and he
in God. And we have come to know and have believed
the love which God has for us. God is love, and the one
who abides in love abides in God, and God abides in him
. . . . We love, because He first loved us.

This love can reduce the potential for frustration. Striving for
self-satisfaction breeds frustration, but because God has met
our basic needs for love, assurance, security and self-worth, we
are no longer chained to the bondage of self-satisfaction. This
freedom gives us patience in our relationship with our spouses.
Our frustration level drops significantly when we are concerned
with others and therefore the potential for anger is lessened.

Our agape love can increase our gratitude as well as our constant awareness and remembrance of God's agape love for us.
An attitude of thankfulness for all of life develops. We are able to
see and concentrate upon the positive qualities and attributes of
our spouses, which we may overlook or take for granted. Our
mind-set and attitudes can be refocused because of the presence
of agape love. Any attitudes of appreciation cause us to respond
with even more love toward our spouses.

Agape love manifests itself with these characteristics. *It is
an unconditional love.* It is not based upon your spouse's performance, but upon your need to share this act with your
spouse. If you don't, your spouse may live with the fear that you
will limit your love if he or she does not meet your expectations.
Agape love is given in spite of how he or she behaves. This form
of real love is an unconditional commitment to an imperfect person.

Agape love is also a transparent love. It is strong enough to
allow your partner to get close to you and inside you. Transparency involves honesty, truth and sharing positive and negative
feelings.

Paul Tournier shared the story of a woman whose mother
gave her this advice: "Don't tell your husband everything: to
maintain her prestige and keep her husband's love, a woman

must retain a certain mystery for him." Tournier commented, "What a mistake! It fails to recognize the meaning of marriage and the meaning of love. Transparency is the law of marriage and the couple must strive for it untiringly at the cost of confessions which are always new and sometimes very hard."[4]

Agape love has a deep reservoir to draw from, so no matter what occurs the love is felt and provides stability during times of stress and conflict.

Agape kindness is servant power. Kindness is love's willingness to enhance the life of another. It is the readiness to move close to another and allow him/her to move close to you. Agape is trying to be content with those things that don't live up to your expectations.

Agape love and philia love need time and attention in order to grow. Your love for your future mate can be a blending of all three kinds of love. Dwight Small describes the process in this way.

> Romantic love diminishes as mature, caring love expands to take its place. For many couples, this is not a dramatic change but a transition so smooth as to be imperceptible. Two people simply emerge from their private cocoon, as it were, into the sunlight of a new life together. Now they understand the darkness and restrictedness of the cocoon of their former privatis.[5]

Test Your Love

Let's think together one more time about your love. Since it is sometimes difficult to really determine if what you are feeling is genuine love, here are several tests for love. In his book, *I Married You,* Walter Trobisch has suggested six of them.

1. *The Sharing Test.* Are you able to share together? Do you want to make your partner happy or do you want to become happy?
2. *The Strength Test.* Does your love give you new strength and fill you with creative energy? Or does it take away your strength and energy?

3. *The Respect Test.* Do you really have respect for each other? Are you proud of your partner?
4. *The Habit Test.* Do you only love each other or do you also like each other and accept each other with your habits and shortcomings?
5. *The Quarrel Test.* Are you able to forgive each other and give in to each other? The ability to be reconciled after a real quarrel must be tested before marriage.
6. *The Time Test.* "Never get married until you have summered and wintered with your partner." Has your love summered and wintered? Have you known each other long enough to know each other well?[6]

Here are four additional tests:

7. *The Separation Test.* Do you feel an unusual joy while in the company of each other? Is there pain in separation?
8. *The Giving Test.* Love and marriage are giving, not getting. Are you in love to give? Are you capable of self-giving? Is this quality of self-giving constantly evident?
9. *The Growth Test.* Is your love dynamic in its growth? Is it progressively maturing? Are the characteristics of Christian love developing?
10. *The Sex Test.* Is there a mutual enjoyment of each other without the constant need of physical expression? If you can't be together without petting, you don't have the maturity and love essential for marriage.[7]

Let's go back to one of the questions I mentioned at the beginning of the chapter. It was, "Why do you love your fiancé?" Consider these reasons one man listed:

Reasons Why I Love Jan

1. Because her educational standards are high. I am of the realization that these standards will be instilled within our children.
2. Because Jan perceives life with such profound insights. She appreciates God's creation.
3. Because Jan makes a conscious and earnest effort to please others, even before herself.

4. Because Jan is able to meet my physical, spiritual and emotional needs. Physical, in that she is able to give warmth and comfort; spiritual, in that she is able to add biblical insights into everyday situations; emotional, in that she is able to be empathetic toward my sensitivities.

5. Because I have the freedom to share my most inward feelings, knowing that I will not be met with rejection, but rather, knowing that Jan will make an earnest effort to understand.

6. Because Jan has learned, and is continually learning, the art of submission without the threat of subserviency.

7. Because she values me. She appreciates my warmth and understanding. She appreciates my efforts to comfort and console her. I love being appreciated.

8. Jan accepts me for who I am, knowing my imperfections, and just as importantly, she is able to constructively work with me to my betterment.

9. Because I really enjoy her company. I enjoy walking and talking with her. We can talk about anything and everything.

10. Because she is open to growth and willing to change.

11. Because of her high moral standard, which will have a positive influence on our relationship.

12. Because of her extreme honesty.

13. Because I wish to give of myself to Jan. To be understanding, gentle, warm, empathetic—being able to listen with an open heart and arms.

Let me share with you the best definition of married love I've ever heard: "Marriage is an unconditional commitment to an imperfect person." What a goal for us to work toward![8] Listen to the words of a wife describing what this involves.

Ideal Marriage: A Choosing to Love

I married a man I respect;
  I have no need to bow and defer.
I married a man I adore and admire;

I don't need to be handed a list entitled
   "how to build his ego" or
"the male need for admiration."
Love, worship, loyalty, trust—these are inside me;
   They motivate my actions.
   To reduce them to rules destroys my motivation.
I choose to serve him
   to enjoy him.
We choose to live together
   and grow together,
      to stretch our capacities for love
         even when it hurts
            and looks like conflict.
We choose to learn to know each other
   as real people,
      as two unique individuals
         unlike any other two.
Our marriage is a commitment to love;
   to belong to each other
      to know and understand
        to care
           share ourselves
             our goals
               interests
                 desires
                   needs
Out of that commitment the actions follow.
Love defines our behavior
   and our ways of living together.
And since we fail to meet not only the demands
   of standards but also the
      simple requirements of love
We are forced to believe in forgiveness
   . . . and grace.[9]

4
COMMITMENT TO CHANGE

Few things in this life remain stable or permanent. Things change. People change. Relationships change. The unspoken assumption that both the marriage relationship and the partners will remain the same is a prelude to trouble. All marriages enter into phases or stages. The changes that occur in these stages are not necessarily good or bad, but they are reality. Here are the typical stages through which most marriages pass:

1. Honeymoon
2. Expectant parenthood
3. Parenthood with preschool children
4. Child rearing
5. Parenthood with adolescents
6. Child launching
7. Empty nest
8. Retirement

Prior to marriage, couples should discuss these stages and how each of them and their relationship will change. This is the first step toward building your marriage—to be aware of the stages of marriage and what to expect during each of them. Knowing what others have experienced helps to make you aware of potential pitfalls and enables you to handle these unexpected events when and if they do occur.

Often changes in our lives come upon us without warning. We are not prepared for them and have not planned what we will do in the event of such changes. But much of the time we can anticipate and control changes. Ignoring the inevitable and refusing to think about and plan for these changes will make adjustment to them even more difficult.

Perhaps there are some potential changes that you would rather not face at this time. You can choose not to plan for the changes in your marriage. You may feel that you want to keep it as it is, that if you do nothing your marriage will change naturally, and only for the better. Then if your marriage does not change for the better, you can blame your spouse.

Some couples react to changes in their relationship by creating distance; they separate or divorce. Often this response comes when each partner believes that the other person is responsible for the trouble in the marriage. Both of these solutions—refusing to plan for changes and creating distances from the marital partner—are the result of believing that change occurs outside of themselves. This belief will hinder growth and positive changes that can take place in marital relationships.

Prepare for Inevitable Changes

We need to expect change in marriage, say David and Vera Mace:

> We need to see marriage in new terms, as a continually growing, continually changing, interaction between a man and woman who are seeking the warmth and richness of the shared life. Marriage has too often been portrayed as two people frozen together side by side, as immobile as marble statues. More accurately, it is the intricate and graceful cooperation of two dancers who through long practice have learned to match each other's movements and moods in response to the music of the spheres.[1]

All changes, whether predictable or intrusive, hold the potential for growth; they are also risky. Untimely or unexpected events upset our plans, their sequence and fulfillment. They bother us because they are thrust upon us, leaving us feeling powerless. We don't like to feel out of control and thus we resist, react negatively or feel overwhelmed instead of seeking creative possibilities in this inevitable situation.

For example, I am a father. I expected to enter the "empty nest" stage of my marriage at about age 48 or 50. And yet at 41—about seven years ahead of schedule—I found myself in that season of life. Matthew, who was expected to be normal and live with us until college, was born severely mentally retarded. At age 11 he was placed in a home for specialized care. The placement was planned but adjustments still had to be made.

Robert Mason, Jr. and Caroline L. Jacobs have this to say:

> Unfortunately, many marriages die prematurely because too many husbands and wives choose to ignore the inescapable fact that people do change.
>
> People can grow apart even when they truly love and care for each other. For some the resistance to change is so deeply ingrained that acceptance of change, even in someone they dearly love, is almost impossible. However, since it is an indisputable fact of life that people do change, and since this is one of the major reasons listed by couples as the source of problems in marriage, couples would do well to explore in depth their ability to adjust to the many changes which are inevitable in the years after marriage.
>
> Difficulties might be anticipated if:
>
> 1. Either person seems locked into a way of thinking or behaving which allows for no difference of opinion or new ideas.
> 2. Either has communicated to the other what he or she wants in a husband or wife and gives the impression that he or she will not tolerate any deviation

from this rigid stance, now or in the future.

3. One of the individuals demonstrates a desire to grow and improve while the other seems determined to maintain the status quo.

4. One or both show a noticeable lack of curiosity or interest in the changes which are occurring around him or her from day to day.

5. Either gets upset easily or acts as if the whole day is ruined if things do not go according to schedule or plans are changed. The individual who is unable to adjust to change before marriage is not likely to be able to adjust to change after marriage.[2]

Any new change carries a time of risk, insecurity and vulnerability. But many of life's events can be planned for in advance—such as having a baby—and can bring security and satisfaction. Some aspects of the various seasons of a marriage are fairly predictable in the changes they bring. These also can be anticipated. As a person moves from his twenties to his thirties, to his forties and fifties he will display characteristics that most people have in common. Becoming parents, having adolescents, the empty nest, the midyears, becoming grandparents and retirement are seasons we are aware of; we know when they are upon us for the most part. Some events, however, come as a surprise and bring tension, pain and unexpected circumstances.

Sudden or Unexpected Changes

In their book *How to Stay Married,* Clark Blackburn and Norman Lobsenz write:

According to family service experts, any sudden change becomes a threat to whatever marital balance has been achieved. It tends to reawaken personal insecurities that the marriage has successfully overcome or held in check. You've noticed how sick people tend to fall back into childish ways—they become terribly dependent, demanding, unreasonable. Similarly some people regress in other kinds of emotional crises. Long-conquered patterns of behavior reassert themselves, at least until the first impact of the shock has been absorbed.[3]

Events occur in our environment that also product stress. A 1971 issue of *Science Digest* reported a study by Eugene S. Pakyel in which 373 people were asked to rate the most "upsetting" events in their lives. The 25 most distressing events (which can induce a depression reaction), from most stressful to least stressful, were:

1. Death of a child
2. Death of a spouse
3. Jail sentence
4. Unfaithful spouse
5. Major financial difficulty
6. Business failure
7. Being fired
8. Miscarriage or stillbirth
9. Divorce
10. Marital separation due to an argument
11. Court appearance
12. Unwanted pregnancy
13. Major illness in the family
14. Unemployment tor a month (Additional studies indicated that four out of five marriages end in divorce when the husband is out of work for nine months or more.)
15. Death of a close friend
16. Demotion
17. Major personal illness
18. Start of an extramarital affair
19. Loss of personally valued objects
20. Lawsuit
21. Academic failure
22. Child married without family approval
23. Broken engagement
24. Taking out a large loan
25. Son drafted[4]

What kind of situations are particularly stressful to you? List three changes or upsetting events that would be the most difficult for you to handle were they to occur.

1.

2.

3.

One of the most critical elements that helps a marriage survive a sudden crisis is the emotional interdependence between the partners. Without this interdependence a sudden upset from the outside can be crippling. Marriages that are strong emotionally tend to become stronger in a crisis. Those that are weak become weaker.

Let's consider a few events that may become crises.

Loss of a Job

When a man loses a job and remains unemployed for a considerable amount of time, a marriage can be disrupted. If his wife has never been employed, the role reversal can be uncomfortable. If the couple has been avoiding conflict issues, the husband's increased presence around the house can force more conflicts. Many men's self-concept is related to their involvement at work and losing a job is a severe blow. Losing his job may lead a man to over-emphasize his authority at home. This is a time when balanced emotional support and honest communication can be a healing influence.

Birth of a Child

The birth of a child can affect both partners negatively unless time and effort have gone into the planning necessary to be parents. Unfortunately, most couples do not plan for the birth of a child. Some husbands become upset by the new expectations placed upon them: less attention from their wives, less sleep and rest, perhaps more work around the house and less spontaneous availability of their wives to go out or entertain.

Many mothers become depressed after the birth of a child. Their depression is called the "four-day blues" or postpartum blues. Many husbands have difficulty handling this kind of depression because they cannot understand why it occurs. Hormonal disturbances or drugs that the woman has taken sometimes contribute to this depression. Physical exhaustion is also a contributing factor.

A woman who is a perfectionist may have difficulty adjusting to the arrival of a noisy, dirty and demanding child. She would like to be the perfect mother with the perfect child and finds coping with reality difficult. Perhaps the wife has had an idealized picture of what having a child would be like and the responsibility begins to weigh heavily upon her. Now that she has a home, a husband, and a child, she may begin to question her ability to handle all of these responsibilities. All of these new responsibilities, coupled with uncertainty, may bring about a change in her self-concept.

Another reason for a prolonged postpartum depression may be that she thinks a mother should feel pride and satisfaction at the birth of a healthy child. When she does not, she begins to question herself and consider herself a failure or a poor mother. Many life changes occur at this time!

Moving to a New Community

Financial strain, selling, renting, redecorating, expending excessive physical energy, losing familiar surroundings, entering new schools or new church, and making new friends are all involved when a family moves to a new community. All of these situations contribute to creating a crisis.

Spouse's or Child's Illness

A spouse's illness can seriously affect the emotional balance of a marriage. If a husband is sick, his wife may feel threatened with the potential emotional and/or financial loss. Again, some dormant conflicts may emerge. If a child is ill, parents become frightened, which causes anxiety for them. Illness can create strain upon a marriage.

Death of a Child

A prevailing assumption is that a couple who loses a child through death draws closer together in their marital relationship. Statistics indicate, however, that the effect of a child's death on the marriage is usually negative. Approximately 80 percent of couples who lose a child in death eventually divorce.

Marriages do not have to die when a child dies. In the midst of intense pain and loss it is possible to reach out to each other. Couples have to *choose* to live again, to activate their faith and share their pain with the Lord. Through this experience the Word of God can help parents gradually hope again. The awareness and application of "my grace is sufficient for thee" becomes evident in time.

Child Leaving Home

A child leaving home changes the balance and roles of the family. If you have three children and now only two are left at home, how will this vacancy affect those who remain? What if he was the tension reliever, the joker and humorist? Who picks up the slack?

What happens when the last child leaves the nest? Is this a time of sadness, emptiness? Many marriages dissolve at this point because the couple must face the emptiness of their marriage which they have been avoiding. Many couples, however, look forward to the time when the last fledgling leaves the nest and they can enjoy their marriage even more. What makes the difference?

The preceding changes are considered major crises. But for some individuals, even minor changes are major upsets. How would you react if:

- Your spouse no longer wanted to go to your favorite restaurant for dinner?
- Your spouse wanted to change a regular family tradition that includes your parents?
- Your spouse announced that a new business opportunity had opened in another state and wanted to move?
- Your spouse quit preparing your favorite dinner?

- Your spouse changed his/her entire style of clothing?
- You lost a $500 investment in a new business through a business reversal?
- Your spouse got rid of your favorite piece of furniture?

How to Cope with Change

Is there a way to lessen the intensity of change so that we suffer less? Yes, there is.

First, be aware of the normality of the process of change. Awareness can relieve some anxiety and guilt for feeling and behaving the way we do.

Second, develop greater flexibility in your daily life-style. Learning to make and accept even minor changes can be a foundation for making larger adjustments.

Third, when major changes are forthcoming, plan for them in advance and learn to rely upon the promises of God's Word.

A few months after our son Matthew was born in 1967, we became aware that his development was quite slow. At eight months of age he began having grand mal seizures. Within a few months we discovered that Matthew had an improper brain formation in addition to brain damage. He was diagnosed as profoundly retarded.

Matthew's presence brought numerous changes and adjustments to all of us. We experienced grief and went through the stages of a severe loss. Joyce and I grew individually in maturity and our Christian life and our marriage were strengthened.

In 1975 we started talking and praying about what was best for Matthew and our family. In 1978 we were led to place Matthew in a private Christian facility for the severely handicapped, where he is progressing very well. We anticipated many of the changes, talked them through, prayed about them and talked about them again. These changes included:

- Three less meals to fix each day
- One or two less loads of wash each day
- No more diapers or Pampers to change each day
- A major topic of our conversation would no longer be there

• A more spontaneous life-style could be developed.

But then other questions arose. Were our self-concepts or feelings about ourselves based on our caring for Matthew? If so, how would placing him in a home affect us? Had we used Matthew in some way to strengthen our feelings of worth? How would we feel about having someone else take care of him and perhaps do a better job? What if he becomes attached to the people at the home more than to us? What if he forgets us? Were we really doing the right thing for Matthew or did we make this decision more for ourselves? Would we experience guilt? Did we like having a person be totally dependent upon us?

Those were questions that we anticipated and worked through. We also were reminded of God's faithfulness in the past and realized that this too was a step of faith. Our adjustment (which included a time of loss, loneliness and hurt) was much easier because we planned, prayed and watched as God continued to work in His unique manner.

Prior to Matthew's entering his new home, we scheduled four different dates for the move. Each time there was a delay—Matthew was sick or there was a funding problem or a change at the home. When Matthew finally entered the home, the transition was very smooth because we had already gone through the emotional transition of having everything ready. We were prepared for the move. We have learned the truth of God's Word: "Thou dost keep him in perfect peace, whose mind is stayed on thee, because he trusts in thee" (Isa. 26:3, *RSV*).

Preparing for Change

The normalcy and potential of change is a message that couples need to hear before they marry. I want you to hear it before any sudden event hits you. Many relationships could avoid the turmoil and disruption caused by unexpected changes if couples were better informed beforehand. The marital journey is compared, by Dr. Mark Lee, to a ride in a New York subway car:

Anyone who has ridden in an old New York subway car will recall his sensation of pitching and rolling as the train raced along work tracks or slowed to a stop in a station. Standing passengers move as one body back and forth with the car's sway and changing velocity. All that prevents a pile-up of bodies on a turn or quick stop are the overhead straps. Almost oblivious to what is happening, passengers grip a strap, automatically tightening and loosening their holds to meet changing situations. In their free hands they hold on for dear life.[5]

Perhaps what we experience in times of change can be likened to a shellfish. A lobster is protected by an extremely hard shell. But as it grows and develops it sheds its old shell to make room for growth. For a while, after the old shell falls off, the lobster is left exposed and vulnerable until a new shell develops.

Hiking in the back country of the Sierras one year, I found myself working along a rock shelf 30 feet above a lake. I was trying to find a way to reach the waterfall at the lake's inlet. At one point—in order to pass around a cliff—I had to relinquish my safe hold on one side of the barrier and almost slither my body across the protruding boulder before I could reach the safety of a new hand hold. For a while I hesitated. I didn't want to give up the safety of my grip for the insecurity of moving a few feet, exposed and insecure, to the new location. But to obtain what I wanted I had to take the risk.

This is often how we feel when we encounter change. But to grow and mature the old must be given up in search of the new. Risk, change and insecurity are positives!

Asked if the love in his marital relationship had changed after 20 years of marriage, a husband replied:

I still feel passion and excitement with my wife. But all of life moves in patterns and cycles, and I think marriages go the same way. A marriage has its dry moments and hot moments, its ups and downs. Most marriages today don't make it. I think the ones that do, survive by going through these changes. As long as you're allowing something to happen within your marriage, then I think there's some chance for its survival. The secret of a good marriage is change. It's gotta move. If it stops, it's dead.[6]

Change in marriage will be inevitable. If we view it realistically we can use it to build positive relationships.

5
COMMITMENT TO UNDERSTAND YOURSELF

We are a people who dream. We have a lifelong pattern of imagining. We dream of the type of person we will become, the type of marriage we will have and the type of parents we will be. And we use these dreams to measure whether we are a success or failure. These dreams or images come from both childhood and adult experiences, and a major adult adjustment is to refashion our dreams to fit reality. If we, as adults, cling to these dreams in the face of a totally opposite reality, we may experience disappointment, rage, depression and turmoil.

Adulthood brings dynamic changes for men and women. You are different today than you were five years ago. What will you be like five years from now? Ten years from now? What will you be doing? Who will you be? What do you want to be at that time? If you could know the answers to these questions now it would make the future easier.

Those Transitional Twenties and Thirties

While I cannot tell you everything you may experience, this chapter gives a preview of some of the more prevalent situations you may expect during your twenties and thirties. The question is, "How will these experiences affect my future life?" If you have already passed this season of your life then you can identify with some of these occurrences and can see how they are affecting you presently. The transition of the forties are a reflection of the influence of the two previous decades.

We begin the venture into adulthood as we are released from adolescence, usually in our twenties. Hopefully, our parents have completed the deparenting process and we are free to move into a new stage of independence and responsibility. For some the move from adolescence to adulthood is like a major earthquake with dramatic upheavals and shifts in personality. For others the transition is less traumatic. No matter how the change occurs the young adult should be in a somewhat steadier, more integrated state than he was in his teens.

Early adulthood is a time of either giving up some past relationships or changing them. Beliefs and dreams have to be altered. Childish fantasies begin to dim, although a certain idealism continues to motivate us. In a sense, life becomes narrower and more focused.

Some pressing decisions must be made during early adulthood which involve time and energy. Both our inner motivations and the outside world pressure the fledgling adult for decisions. These decisions include:

1. Should I attend college or seek employment?
2. If I go to school what courses should I take?
3. Can I handle work and school too? What about the pressure?
4. Who pays the bill if I go to school? (This could perpetuate dependency upon your parents.)
5. After college, what is next? Employment or graduate school?
6. What about a relationship with another person? Should I pursue casual dating, serious dating or marriage? Should I wait a while?
7. What will I miss out on because of any of my choices?
8. What do I really want to do that would be a reflection of me as a person? Who am I and how should this be expressed?
9. What will give me the greatest security? What will create the greatest insecurity?
10. What is God's will for my life?

Questions such as these continue and continue. We become increasingly aware that wrong choices can bring lasting consequences. The childhood belief that there is no time limit is over.

The great task of the twenties is really, "What do I do with this period of my life?" Choice is the screaming theme. Dr. Daniel Levinson of Yale University labels this time period "The Dream." During early adulthood the young adult attempts to make his dream become a reality and by his own choice. It is not a peaceful time, as Maggie Scarf suggests:

> The newly emerged self of the early twenties can, nevertheless, be compared to a relatively recent geological formation. It is patently there, and has its own contours and outline; it has its dimensions, height, circumference, and breadth. Still, it is subject to underground shudders and tremblings; it is newly formed and not settled; it can still shift in its shape and its structure. It may still experience great aftershocks. For, whether or not the adolescent transformation has been perceived as a time of earth-shaking alterations, it has—as earthquakes do—involved the release of accumulated strains and pressures at the very core of one's being.[1]

A person in his twenties is beginning to formulate his dream or vision of what he wants in life and how to pursue it. He is building his life structure. Some people are foresighted; they are able to lay meaningful foundations for the future. Others are quite short-sighted—there is still a vagueness about their dream.

One way to bring a dream into focus is to ask yourself, "What kind of a life do I want to lead as an adult?" This can turn a vague fantasy into, as Levinson describes it, "imagined possibility that generates excitement and vitality."[2]

Two Primary Dream Pursuits

What is your dream? Two major dreams that adolescents formulate are (1) the vocational dream and (2) the marital dream.

Your main task during your twenties is to clarify and define your dreams and then develop a plan to attain them. Some questions you may ask yourself are: "Where does the will of God enter in?" "What does He want for me at this particular time of my life?" "Where does 'Seek ye first the kingdom of God and his righteousness' enter in?" (see Matt. 6:33). "Am I seeking a vocation or my future spouse in order to *establish* my adequacy or out of a *sense* of adequacy?" And perhaps most important, "Does this dream come from within me or has it been forced upon me?" This last question is particularly critical in your choice of a vocation.

Sometimes a vocational dream is influenced by economic factors, a lack of other opportunities, the wishes of parents, a desire to please a fiancé, personality defects or even because the person possesses a unique talent that could become an occupation. Whatever the motivation, it is possible for you to go into an occupation, be very successful and yet be bored and discouraged. Many people in our country are in this position.

Pursuing a wrong dream in your twenties and building your life around it will bring consequences you must live with for many years. Your marriage and your total outlook on life will be affected by the choice and pursuit of your vocational dream. However, it is well to remember that the vocational choices you make now are not necessarily irrevocable. Change at this point and in the future is usually possible.

When the time comes for you to pursue your dream, you may do one of two things. First, because you want to get the whole thing over with and you feel that you will have a firm, secure future, you may make some strong, definite commitments that are virtually set in concrete. In doing this you may overly resist and feel threatened by change or intrusions from the outside. If you do not take enough time to carefully consider your choice of occupation, however, you will encounter frustration in the future. You will feel locked in and restricted. It is as though a person were building a very straight, predictable railroad toward a destination and, at the same time, he erects a wall on both sides of the track, eliminating all alternative directions.

The other tendency is to continue to explore and experiment

without a definite commitment. Although this gives you the opportunity to change directions more easily, if this exploration continues throughout the twenties, you may turn into a vocational transient. Some people make numerous changes in vocation, relationships and residences, but there must come a time of settling down.

In a sense, the person in his twenties must walk a tightrope between exploration and settling down. It is interesting to evaluate your own particular pattern as it is reflected in other areas of life besides your vocation. In your man/woman relationships, your spiritual life and in other areas, are you rigidly set or continually open to change?

There is no guarantee about your choice of occupation. Those who make the commitment too early may learn to live with regret. Those who delay their commitment or never commit themselves at all, lose much of the satisfaction of personal fulfillment.

Also during the twenties most people commit themselves to marriage. As it is in choosing an occupation it is in choosing a spouse: a person often makes his choice before he is ready to know exactly what he wants and how to achieve it.

What happens if you marry at the start of your transition from adolescence to adult? You find yourself learning to separate from your parents, trying out the new adult world and adapting to a spouse all at the same time. Sometimes early marriage (ages 17-22) perpetuates difficulties with parents and you end up retaining some of your childish qualities. The new husband and wife may both feel extra strain at this time because they are both emerging.

He or she may have had little experience in forming peer relationships with members of the opposite sex. The mate may become a tool to help the person relinquish his or her relationship with parents and become an adult.

If you wait to marry until you are between the age of 22 to 28, being married can either contribute to or detract from your personal development. Your marital partner should be a person who will share your dreams and who is willing to let you share his or her plans and dreams.

However, if you reach your thirties and still aren't married, you may experience pressure from friends, parents and even business associates to marry. You may try to conform and make your life "normal" without having resolved some of your inner conflicts.

No matter at what stage a couple experiences marriage, there will be issues and conflicts to resolve. Both the man and woman must continue to develop personally as well as together. They can no longer rely upon their society, culture, family or even their commitment to their faith to keep their marriage together. Marriages receive less outside support today than they used to because of the change in values, culture, divorce laws and an emphasis upon selfishness and individualism. Greater effort and commitment on the part of each are needed. Greater commitment to the fidelity and permanency concepts of Scripture is also needed.

A lasting relationship is more possible if both partners continue to grow and develop. If the husband uses his wife to further the attainment of his dream and in the process she loses her own dream, her growth will be stifled and eventually both will be disappointed. For example, a medical student marries and his wife supports him for years in the pursuit of his dream. She foregoes her own advancement, education and intellectual development. Soon the children arrive. He is into his 80-hour-a-week practice and becomes acquainted with a woman who is freer, less restricted and more intellectually stimulating than his wife. He decides to change partners.

Or a man may choose to marry only because in his profession a family man is more acceptable. In this case he may see his wife and children as necessary accessories.

Sometimes a marriage relationship hinders the pursuit of a man's dream. His wife may have no interest in his dream and may even prevent him from attaining it. Her own dream may be complementary, different or antagonistic. Any of these conditions can affect the success of the marriage.

If a woman sees herself in the traditional roles of wife and mother, she may derive her identity from her husband and what he does. She sees her husband as her protector and turns her whole being over to him. She continues to support *his* dream as long as he gives sufficient attention to her and their family, and as long as she feels needed by him and their children. She probably believes that men are attracted primarily to physical beauty and helplessness. But as she ages, her physical attractiveness may fade and her husband may grow weary of her "helplessness." By her thirties and forties she may be needed less and less by her husband and family and she may be forced to seek out her own identity.

If a woman has been overly dependent on her husband and decides to change, her husband may feel threatened, especially if the change costs him something. He accepts it better if it benefits him. She could begin to believe that her husband is the obstacle to her growth. In actuality, it may just be that he is not giving her the encouragement she desires from him.

It is not uncommon for a woman in her late thirties or early forties to experience an identity crisis. She may become disillusioned with her traditional role; she may resent her caretaker husband. If she decides to develop some independence and pursue a career, she may face a number of obstacles. Job availability may be limited. Or if she finds a job, she may find the role of both a career woman and a homemaker a strain. Some women are a bit fearful of the feelings of competition and power within them which have lain dormant for so many years. Accepting these and using them in a creative way, both within the home and in a career, can be a freeing experience.[3]

But no matter what age a person chooses to marry, he or she will find certain problems—as well as a great many advantages—in becoming adjusted to married life.

Marriage in the Early Years

In the midst of developing their own personal lives, a man and a woman marry. The romantic idealism eventually turns to the question, "Will we make it together?" Great expectations and hopes are mixed with fears, anxieties and surprises. A host of new and unexpected events come into their lives. Those which are expected or anticipated will be handled fairly smoothly but the surprises can be disruptive. This is why extensive and thorough premarital preparation with a minister or counselor is such a necessity. As there are stages and phases to work through in one's own life, there are also important stages and phases to work through in the first few years of marriage.

Three Important Tasks

The ffirst task is to define what a "wife" is and what a "husband" is. It is important that each retains his/her individual identity while drawing close together as a couple. A marriage relationship is meant to be a freeing-up relationship and never a confinement. Each person is freed-up to develop uniqueness and spiritual giftedness in his or her own way, and join these to give the marital relationship strength and greater potential. This may mean breaking loose from preconceived images each one has of what a wife or husband should be. If couples cannot allow each other to develop, grow and be creative in defining new roles, the conflict will be intense. As one author so vividly puts it, "Both of you will wind up drilling holes in your own marriage before it has left the shore."[4]

A second task is to create a new relationship with your parents. You need to be independent from them yet retain a close, loving relationship. You must break the parent-child ties and reestablish them in an adult-adult relationship. A person needs to complete the separation process from his parents for a marriage to develop. One must "leave" in order to properly "cleave," as it states in Genesis 2:24. By having made peace with one's parents and separating completely, a man/woman can be at peace with his/her own self and thus with a marriage partner.

A third task is to develop the romantic love of courtship into a love based upon steady commitment. Before you marry you may be drawn to your friend because of a specific character trait which you see as a strength. But when you marry you may find that this "strength" begins to bother you. You begin to view it as a weakness rather than a strength and you want the person to change. This character trait, however, is an expression of his or her personality. If it bothers you it needs to be discussed but not attacked as a weakness. Labeling a behavior as a weakness does little to bring about change.

The love which is needed to stabilize a marriage is the type of love God displays to each of us—an unconditional commitment to an imperfect person. This takes energy and effort. It means caring about the other person as much as you care about yourself. Mel Krantzler describes what marital love actually means.

> Marital love requires the ability to put yourself in your partner's place, to understand that the differences that divide you are the differences of two unique personalities, rather than betrayals of your hopes and dreams. The unconditional willingness of each of you to understand and resolve these differences through the sharing of your deepest feelings, concerns, attitudes and ideas is a fundamental component of marital love. Postponement of your need for instant gratification when your partner feels no such need; sharing the struggle to triumph over adversities as well as sharing the joys and delights of being together; nurturing each other in defeat caused by forces beyond our control and renewing each other's courage to prevail in the face of despair; carrying necessary obligations and responsibilities as a flower rather than as a hundred-pound knapsack; acknowledging the everyday value of your partner in a look, a smile, a touch of the hand, a voiced appreciation of a meal or a new hair style, a spontaneous trip to a movie or a restaurant; trusting your partner always to be there when needed; knowing that he or she always has your best interests at heart even when criticism is given; loyalty and dedication to each other in the face of sacrifices that may have to be made—all of these are additional components of marital love that courtship knows little about.[5]

These are just a few of the tasks a couple faces in the early years of their marriage.

The Family Life Cycle

The level of marital satisfaction fluctuates at different stages of the family life cycle. Numerous studies have been conducted in an attempt to determine changes during the cycle. Figure 1, which is based upon several research studies, indicates changes in satisfaction at seven nuclear family stages among typical middle-class couples. Many couples will reflect this trend while others will vary considerably. Did your parents follow this trend? Do you think you will follow this trend? Considering the potential adjustments that occur at each stage is one means of identifying the stress and disruption of a marital relationship.

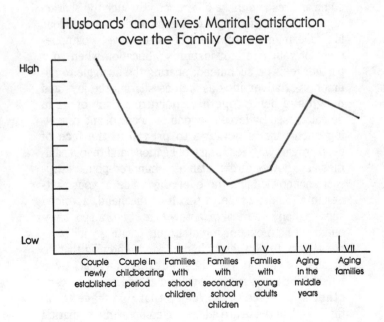

Husbands' and Wives' Marital Satisfaction over the Family Career

NUCLEAR FAMILY STAGES
Figure 1

Jane Aldous describes the fluctuation that occurs in marital satisfaction:

> Marriages may be made in heaven, as the popular saying goes, but their maintenance occurs in an earthly setting. The emotional euphoria with which most marriages start is eroded over time by establishing daily routines, by growing irritations from constant association, by competing attractions of jobs and children, and by coping with the multitudinous problems, both large and small, that family life in an industrialized society entails. Fortunate couples develop an intimate understanding unique to the relationship that replaces the raptures of the first period of the marital career.[6]

Many predictable changes occur as couples proceed through the various stages of the family life cycle. All of these changes have the potential for drawing a couple closer together. However, some of these changes unfortunately become cripplers of the marriage.

Adjustments you and your spouse will need to make include need fulfillment, adjusting to differentness, establishing goals, expressing emotions, communicating styles, decision making, power structuring, creating roles, adjusting to family background and in-laws, just to mention a few.

As you begin the family life cycle, problems will develop if you:

1. Were not adequately prepared for marriage
2. Are unable to handle disappointment, hurt and suffering
3. Are unaware of the effects of the various stages of the family life cycle on your marriage
4. Lack understanding concerning you and your spouse's striving for identity and intimacy. Identity is the sense of "who I am." Intimacy is a relationship of closeness, total honesty and trust.

Identity vs. Intimacy_____

A man builds his identity through his occupation or profession. Many men pursue goals of making a good living and finding a good life, which prove to them that they are adequate and of worth. (This typically male process is undergoing some change, however, as many women are now pursuing careers and professions.) Because their identities are built in this manner, men devote their time and energy to work. The marital relationship often takes a secondary position. When couples marry, the timing is such that most men are just at the point of establishing themselves in their line of work. Their main task at this time is establishing identity through their work. At the onset of marriage a wife is seeking to build an intimate relationship with her husband. This is where frustration may occur: identity vs. intimacy.

Underlying part of many wives' strong emphasis upon intimacy is their own striving for building their sense of identity. Often they build an identity through their husband or family. (This typically female process is undergoing some change, too, as many women are now being employed outside of the home and some marital roles are changing.)

Many wives become discouraged after a few years of marriage because the intimate relationship with their husband does not develop as expected. Thus, in time a wife may turn her efforts for intimacy toward the children. Perhaps this accounts for why many mothers find it so difficult to let go of the children when they are old enough to leave the nest.

If this situation continues—the husband building an identity through work and the wife building intimacy and identity through the children—a crisis will eventually occur. Many husbands in their forties realize they have reached the end of the line for upward progress in their work. There is nowhere else to go, so their goals begin to change. They may now turn back to their wives with a desire to build intimacy. But they may be in for a shock, because many wives, after the children leave home, begin to consider how their own identities have developed. They may be deciding to complete their own education or to pursue a career. Their desire for an intimate relationship with their husbands is not very intense after so many years of no reciprocation on his part.

Let's continue to look at some specific aspects of the family life cycle that can bring either conflict or creative change to a marriage.

Beginning a Family

The arrival of a baby marks the beginning of a new family structure and even a new marital outlook. The novice father and mother establish new patterns of behavior, discover new joys and suffer new stresses. They begin to notice greater uncertainties and fears. Parenting is risky.

Many family study experts say that the birth of the first child is a major crisis for many couples. Why? Because they probably spent more time preparing to get their driver's license than they did preparing for parenthood. Most couples have only a vague idea of what is entailed in the task of parenthood let alone the changes that occur in the marital relationship. One of the biggest adjustments is how to integrate this new person into the family so all three lives are enhanced. There is one guarantee that a child brings with his or her arrival: the guarantee that his or her presence will *not* bring instant happiness or solve marital problems. A child is a bottomless pit of needs and demands. Often a couple will see their child as an enemy because of their own frustration and inability to cope with these changes.

Being a parent is like being an astronaut. No matter how much you are told, how much training and instruction you receive, your own experience can't be predicted: it will be an uncharted course.

And parenthood is like swimming. Some people plunge in without thinking and do a beautiful backstroke; others barely manage a "survival float"; still others can't do even that. They have to call for help.

The birth of a child tests the identities of both parents. Husbands and wives by this time have found ways to build their identities through success in certain performance-oriented tasks, jobs or skills. When the child arrives, the qualities they feel they possess are soon tested. If they are successful in this new venture, they are satisfied that they made a wise decision. But if either the results are negative or their anticipated needs are not fulfilled through parenthood, their identity may suffer. If they depend on positive feedback concerning their role as a parent and it doesn't come, their self-esteem may begin to diminish.

Responding to a child is different from responding to adults in the career world where there are definite and specific guidelines for communication. There the end result is not only immediate in many cases but there is equal and free communication. When a child is involved, especially a very young child, there is little direct communication. A parent's confidence in knowing how to handle situations can erode.

Picture yourself in the bind of many formerly employed mothers. You had a degree of independence and accomplishment in your job. Now you have exchanged your job for motherhood. Often you feel insecure and indecisive in your new role. You receive little assurance that what you are doing is best. The feelings of competence you had when you were employed diminish and your ability to accomplish anything may seem to diminish also. Thus your identity begins to erode. The husband's support and involvement definitely must act as a stable force during this time.

Having a child has the effect of making a woman become selfless and more concerned about the care of another than she was before. To some degree she must rely more on her husband than she did before. As she takes care of another, she needs to be taken care of herself, whether she wants to be or not. In a healthy relationship this need has little or no lessening effect on one's sense of identity.

The new role of motherhood often does away with some of the wishes and desires she can no longer pursue. "Abandon yourself for the good of another" is the maxim she has heard from her parents, church or friends. Following this advice she encounters conflict; for in not meeting her own needs and wishes sufficiently, she has less to give to the child and her fear of being a "bad mother" intensifies.

When you dream about children and being a parent, you fantasize about yourself and your child-to-be. You dream about the type of parent you want to be and the type of child you want to have. Fantasizing is normal; but are the images you see in your dreams realistic? Are they grounded in realistic expectations or are they only wishful thinking? Do these dreams help you fulfill your own desires?

Most couples who experience any preparation at all for parenthood do so minimally during the nine months of pregnancy. And most mothers do more reading and discussing than fathers do.

We spend many years preparing for our vocations and in some instances work into them gradually. We spend, on the average, six months to four years becoming acquainted with our spouses prior to marriage and this relationship gradually grows and develops. Not so with parenthood! We are aware that the child is coming, and then abruptly—a minute later it seems—this new stranger is alive, loud and demanding.[7]

There are numerous challenges to meet. It is important for both a wife and husband to see the child for who he or she is. The child is neither a sexual rival nor a substitute for either spouse. Each spouse needs to develop flexibility to meet his partner's needs in a new way. Expanding the ability to express frustrations, feelings and even delaying some need-satisfaction will be a major step. Realizing that the initial draining schedule of a newborn does not last forever will help you keep things in perspective.

Pregnancy is a time for the creation of new images. A couple begins to think of themselves as "an expecting couple." They learn to accept the pregnancy which involves starting to accept a new role. When a baby arrives the couple begins to form an attachment to the child. This is a process which occurs over time. As the child grows the parents learn to accept the responsibility of being an authority. They must also become teachers and resource specialists for their children, which continues through the teen years.

The task of parenting becomes more complex because of three additional factors: (1) each parent is going through his own individual growth and change process; (2) the couple is working out their own relationship; (3) if there is more than one child, parents have multiple parental roles.

For example, with one child you move through various

stages such as accepting the pregnancy, becoming the parent of a two-year-old, a four-year-old, a six-year-old, an eight-year-old, etc. With one child, a parent proceeds through his own adjustments progressively one step at a time. But now add a second child when the first one is four years old. Now the parents are parents of a newborn and a four-year-old—two roles at once. Four years later, the third child arrives. Now the adjustment involves an eight-year-old, a four-year-old and a newborn. It is true that the second or third child is easier because we now have some experience behind us. But additional children are difficult because attention, time and energy are divided.

The Two-Career Family

When there is economic strain the marriage is a prime target for the never-enough-money conflict. The job becomes the prime concern. It is becoming more common for both husband and wife to work. In the 1980s, in more than 19 million U.S. families, both husband and wife are breadwinners. For many it takes two paychecks just to survive economically. Many of these women do not have adequate skills for a well-paying job so they qualify for jobs that are dull and routine. They worry about being laid off if they are unskilled or if they were recently hired. They still discover biases against them as women in a number of professions and the rat race of competition in some companies.

In many families both partners choose to work. They are career-oriented rather than job-oriented. Many women are not completely fulfilled by the role of wife and mother. They have skills for which somebody (probably parents) invested $30,000-$40,000 for four years of college. And now they are crying to be used.

Some women attempt to develop themselves in both work and marriage simultaneously. This can heighten a woman's inner tensions considerably, for the role expectations are opposite in these two areas of life. For example, what would happen in the career world if the woman were warm, emotional, expressive, noncompetitive, supportive? What would happen in her marriage if she were controlling, pushing, self-assertive, competitive, dominant, etc? It is difficult to shift roles. She has to create two different lives at once! Many women decide that it is better to remove themselves from one of these roles. They either quit their job or their marriage. Men do not encounter this problem because they are expected to exhibit the same characteristics in both marriage and occupation, so their tension and ambivalence are less.

Although the economic burden may be lightened if both partners work at their chosen careers, other problems can arise. One of the biggest problems for two-career families is, who does the housework? One husband, whose wife also worked, began to keep track of the family's use of time. He discovered that he spent an average of 45 minutes a day doing household chores. Their two sons each spent 15 minutes a day and his wife spent six hours every evening. Each had his own set of complaints about the time allotment. The outcome was that the husband and sons took on a much greater share of the household chores to the satisfaction of everyone.

There is one positive potential available if a husband would take advantage of it. Because his wife is also working he does not have to moonlight. Therefore, he can spend more time with his children and create deeper bonds with them. A father must be involved with his children. In fact, Scripture has more to say about the role of a father than a mother. By intimate involvement with his children he can learn to be a more caring and sensitive person. A husband committed to his wife cares and encourages her and is more likely to share household duties. But most men do not become that involved at home with or without children. The stress of shuffling chores may be more than he expected. If the husband refuses to help, resentment and distance soon appear in their relationship and they begin to reinforce each other in a negative manner. Soon their commitment is to their career rather than to each other and their marriage. The husband's desire as to whether she remains a housewife or is employed outside the home is a major factor. If he approves there is likely to be higher marital adjustment than if he disapproves.

If both of you are employed outside the home, marriage will be a challenge. Maintaining your relationship in a loving, close manner will take constant effort. Your response to the following questions can help you decide whether or not you will respond constructively to this challenge. Even if one of you works at home and the other one away, answer as many of these questions as are applicable. Read the questions aloud to your fiancé and discuss each one. Do this again a year after your marriage.

Will you tell each other what happened during your working day?

Will you really listen and care about what has happened to your spouse on the job?

Will only one person ask or tell the other?

Will you refuse to share your concerns about your job because you think your spouse won't understand the problems you are facing at work?

Will you be too embarrassed to tell your spouse if your boss reprimanded you or that you are terrified about making a presentation at a company meeting?

Will you try to put yourself in your spouse's shoes and understand that what might prove to be no problem to you might be a great problem to your partner, requiring your helpful feedback?

Will you admire your spouse's strengths on the job as you would a colleague's, or are you even now secretly envious of those qualities?

Will you feel you are entitled to a greater say in family economic decisions and in household management because you may earn more money than your spouse?

Do you really like the fact that your spouse is going to work?

Do you now take pride in your spouse's professional competency for his or her sake as well as your own?

Do you secretly think you would like it better if your wife greeted you at home every evening with a clean house, refreshments and a hot dinner?

Will you really do your full share of the housework without continual prodding from your wife or without feeling argumentative and resentful because you feel you are always getting the short end of the stick?

Will you view helping your wife entertain her clients as important as her helping you entertain yours?

How will you feel if your wife makes more money than you? If she already is making more money, do you have mixed feelings about that fact? Do you talk to her about your feelings?

Will you feel that you are in competition with your husband regarding who has the best job and who makes the most money? If so, is the feeling one of healthy competitiveness as in a track race or a feeling of guilt or anger because you are competing with him?

Will you do more than your fair share of the housework rather than hold your husband to his end of the bargain because you don't want to make waves?

If your husband makes a larger salary than you, will you feel guilty when you spend money on yourself because you believe you are spending "his" money?

Will you allow your husband's purchasing desires to take priority over your own because he makes more money than you do?

Will you feel you are entitled to less decision-making power in your household because your husband makes more money than you do?

Will you label the total income you and your husband make "our" joint income or do you regard the earnings of each of you separately as a measure of the power each of you brings to your marriage?

How would you feel if you made more money than your husband? If you are making more money now, do you feel guilty or secretive about sharing that fact with friends?

Will you consider your wife's/husband's job a "safety net"?

Today there are numerous life-style options available for a woman from which she can choose. Her own mother probably didn't have much choice; her role was already written in tradition. The dilemma today for women is, "Am I making the right choice?" And this question sometimes haunts them. They feel inward pressure based upon a mixture of beliefs of what a "good mother" is. Pressure comes from friends, church, interpretation of Scripture, parents and other sources. But the internal personal questioning of whether she is doing the right thing may be the greatest plague.

Part of the dilemma comes from the inward screaming of two sets of needs. For example, many women earlier in their lives have the need to develop the career part of their personality. Once this is established the need of the nurturing mother comes to the forefront. Both needs are normal but how does she handle both? Is she to give up one for the other? Can she fulfill both at the same time? A parent who works is no less a parent than one who is at home constantly. With a supportive and encouraging husband, careful planning and proper selection of child care, many couples do work out this type of life-style.

Whether both parents work because of economic necessity or a career choice, they need to resolve their own attitudes. Guilt and questioning must be put to rest so they can give themselves to their tasks with all their energy in a positive way. They also need to learn to handle spoken and unspoken disapproval from outsiders—even if it means occasionally challenging outside reaction.

Couples today need greater freedom in their choice of a life-style than they did 50 years ago. Roles and pressures have changed. The myths of children becoming delinquent and marriages ending in divorce at a greater rate when the mother is employed are just that—myths. The facts do not support them. As I counsel young couples preparing to marry I wonder how they will make it financially today without both being employed for some part of their marriage. They are not seeking a standard of living that is lavish and unrealistic—they simply want to survive.

We all know of couples who both work or have careers and it has created problems. There are many pressures and problems to work through when they have children. But many make the adjustments quite well.

What will you do?

Where Are You in the Life Cycle

Where are you in this vignette of the twenties and thirties? Is it yet to come or has it been? What will be the results or what have the results been?

It is important for men and women at some point in time, to take an inventory of their goals and their identity. Both need to thoughtfully answer questions such as:

1. Do my goals have meaning for me at this time of life?
2. Do my vocational goals or my occupation give me identity and meaning in life?
3. Are my goals realistic and do I have the ability to attain them?
4. How do my goals relate to the Word of God?
5. How do my vocational goals affect my marriage?
6. What is the goal that I have set five years from now in the following areas of my life: (1) vocational, (2) spiritual, (3) marital, (4) family, (5) recreational?

Building Your Self-Concept

This is a serious and heavy chapter. It was meant to be, and hopefully you have looked at yourself in a new light.

We all seek stability, fulfillment, identity and adequacy. This is normal. But it doesn't come from work, relationships or parenthood. It comes from who God is, how He sees us and what He has done for us. Allowing God to have a prominent place in our lives will ease our striving and give us meaning.

The bedrock for our identity is the *fact* that we are created by the hand of God in His image. Like God, we have great intellectual capacities. We are able to amass vast amounts of knowledge and use this information to make complex decisions. Like God, we also have the capacity for self-determination. We can plan ahead, foresee results and make major choices that affect our destiny. We also have the capacity for language and we have great creative ability. We are able to explore nature, produce new inventions and create great works of art. We can use our genius for the service of mankind.

But the image of God goes deeper still. We have a moral nature that enables us to deal with spiritual and ethical matters. God built into Adam and Eve an inherent goodness. They were not morally neutral computers; their moral nature was stamped into the center of their being by the hand of God. We know that

God was pleased with His creation because the book of Genesis states that He "saw all that He had made, and behold, it was very good" (Gen. 1:31, *NASB*).

Jesus Christ invites us to come to Him by faith, believing that He will accept us as we are into His family. "But as many as received Him, to them He gave the right to become children of God, even to those who believe in His name: who were born not of blood, nor of the will of the flesh, nor of the will of man, but of God" (John 1:12-13, *NASB*).

When we have the assurance that we are special because of God's unconditional love, we no longer need to constantly strive to create our own identity.

All of us want to feel competent and worthwhile and to belong. What is it like to belong? It is the awareness of being wanted, accepted, cared for and enjoyed. Often we gain this through performance and achievements at work.

Worthiness is feeling that "I am good"; "I count"; "I am all right." People feel worthy when they do what they think they should. This sense is confirmed when we know that others have positive feelings toward us. We look for their endorsement of our actions. A feeling of worthiness is related to a sense of being right and doing right in our eyes and in the eyes of others. It is important to determine who the people are whose response we are seeking. At work it is probably our employer or fellow employees. When do you feel most worthy? Who are the significant people from whom you desire acceptance?

Competence is a feeling of adequacy. It is feeling "I can"; "I have the ability or strength to do it." Our feeling of adequacy is built upon present as well as past accomplishments. It is based upon the achievement of goals and ideals we have set for ourselves. If I base it upon unrealistic standards or the feedback of others, I will find instability. But if I base it upon what God has done for me, it is possible.

You and I have been accepted with an unconditional acceptance even though we are imperfect. "Therefore if any man is in Christ, he is a new creature; the old things passed away; behold, new things have come" (2 Cor. 5:17, *NASB*). We are God's new creation—we are His workmanship. The one who had the only perfect self-concept, Jesus Christ, is now our model. Our sense of being somebody comes through our relationship with Him. "Put on the new self who is being renewed to a true knowledge according to the image of the One who created him" (Col. 3:10, *NASB*).

Because of our position in Christ we know that we are accepted by God. We belong to Him. "He hath made us accepted in the beloved" (Eph. 1:6, *KJV*). Because God has forgiven us of our sins, we can say with conviction that we are good and worthwhile. "Therefore having been justified by faith, we have peace with God through our Lord Jesus Christ" (Rom. 5:1, *NASB*). And if God and Jesus Christ are with us at all times then we know we are not inferior or inadequate. We have a complete identity.

Dr. Lloyd Ahlem in *Do I Have to Be Me?* clearly summarizes what God has done for us:

> The writers of Scriptures are careful to point out that when God looks at you in Jesus Christ, He sees you as a brother to His own Son. Because of the work of Christ, all of the ugliness of humanity is set aside. God has absolutely no attitude of condemnation toward man. You are worth all of God's attention. If you were the only person in the whole world, it would be worth God's effort to make Himself known to you and to love you, He gives you freely the status and adequacy of an heir to the universe.
>
> This is agape love, the unmerited, unconditional favor of God for man. We achieve our adequacy through this unceasing love. We do not become sufficient, approved or adequate; rather we are declared to be such! When we believe this, we become achievers and humanitarians as an effect, a by-product of our new-found selves.[9]

God's love fulfills our need for competence and identity! "Seek ye first the kingdom of God, and his righteousness; and all these things shall be added unto you" (Matt. 6:33, *KJV*).

6
COMMITMENT TO EVALUATE EXPECTATIONS AND DEVELOP GOALS

The setting and attainment of goals in marriage is one of the most neglected essentials for marital growth. The manner in which a marriage develops and what it reflects is a couple's choice. If you have set well-defined marital goals and have developed strategies and plans to attain your goals, your relationship will continually grow.

Common Marital Expectations

Before you set goals for your marriage, you need to think about your expectations for marriage. We all enter marriage assuming that certain events will transpire and that our relationships will develop in a certain way. These expectations often remain unspoken, even after we are married. Because our spouse is unaware of them, often they are not fulfilled.

Most marital journeys begin with high romantic intensity. As couples approach marriage they usually have only a superficial awareness of each other's wants, needs and expectations. During this time (and unfortunately for many, even after marriage) the least important needs are the ones that get attention.

At the same time, without checking it out with the other, each partner enters marriage assuming that certain events will transpire just the way he or she imagines: "We will visit *my* mother each year on vacation"; "My husband will be home every evening"; "My wife will not work while our children are young"; "We will live in one place and not move around the country," etc. Also the partners imagine that their relationship will develop in a certain way: "We will always be polite to each other"; "My husband will be the spiritual leader in our home"; "My wife will handle the household budget," etc.

Philip Yancy, in his excellent book *After the Wedding,* says that one of the reasons for a sudden drop in marital satisfaction after the honeymoon is adjustments to married life.

Why can't couples predict adjustments before they get married? We've already seen that their romantic perspectives often blind them. Also, there are adjustments in habits they would not know about before marriage (he tosses and turns at night; she hangs pantyhose in the bathroom; he throws tools into messy, disorganized drawers). These can usually be worked out by compromise.

The real tough problems of adjustment come when partners have different expectations about marriage. What if a wife is used to big birthday celebrations and elaborate Christmas decorations and the husband isn't? What about a husband who expects a seductive, affectionate wife who will hang on him publicly—and he finds she's physically aloof? Though hints of these differences appear in courtship, often the huge gulf does not yawn open until after marriage, when the two are thrust together for 16 hours a day, not just when they want to be together.

Does the husband expect the wife to forfeit a career to be housewife and mother? Does the wife expect the husband to be a career climber? Does the wife expect the husband to keep a well-running, clean car? Who should clean the garage? Who is to take the initiative in sex?

If your expectations differ, conflict will result.[1]

Of course, many times these expectations remain unspoken; yet when they are not realized, marital disruption occurs. While most of these expectations are desires—ideal situations— rather than necessities, they still play an important part in marital happiness. What are some of the more prevalent expectations that are nearly guaranteed to go unmet? Let's think of some. I've listed a few to get you started.

Unrealistic Expectations

One of the most common unrealistic expectations is that *the marriage relationship will always be just the way it was in the early days of marriage.* But change will occur. Unfortunately, it overwhelms many individuals and couples, especially if the change is negative or unexpected.

Another expectation, somewhat related to the first, is that *honeymoon fever can be maintained or recaptured.* But life is not static. The additional tasks and responsibilities of marriage and parenting make this expectation unrealistic. Yet, although the honeymoon excitement wanes, the love experienced later in marriage can be a deeper love.

A third unrealistic expectation involves *narcissistic mind reading.* "If my spouse loves me, he or she will know what my needs are and do everything he or she can to meet them." A subtle corollary to this is, "If this doesn't occur, then you don't love me." It would be nice if we were all mind-readers, but such an expectation is unrealistic.

Fourth, *we demand sameness in our partner:* "We should be the same, think the same, do the same things." If the spouse is different, something is wrong. However, if we expect our partner to think and act just as *we* think and act, we will quickly become disillusioned. The dissimilarity we observe creates anxiety and insecurity because "If my partner is different, then perhaps I might have to change."

Abraham Schmitt describes the situation this way:

> In the midst of the marital struggle the honeymoon dream vanishes, and the despair over the old relationship comes up for reexamination. Suddenly each spouse turns his eyes away from the partner, and looks inwardly and asks, "What am I doing to my partner? What is wrong with me? What am I misunderstanding? What must I do to rescue this marriage?" If honestly asked the answers are not far behind: "I really married my wife because of her difference. It is not my job to

make her over, but rather to discover and to value that difference. But before I can do that I must accept my difference and I really need her to help me discover my uniqueness. My task is not to mold her into a beautiful vase, but to participate with her to discover that beautiful vase even as we discover it in me. How arrogant of me to think I could shape another human being! How humble it makes me to realize that I need to yield to another and thereby be changed! Our relationship will change both of us—in a process of being shaped into a form far more beautiful than either could imagine.[2]

Demanding sameness in a partner stifles individuality and creates bondage. Only when a person gives up this expectation can a marriage begin to grow.

Finally, some couples enter marriage *expecting to have problems* because of their differences. Such couples believe that having marital problems is a predetermined fact. They focus on their differences whether or not those differences are really a problem. In such cases they should ask themselves, "What would it be like if I were married to someone just like me? Would I like it?" Who wants to be married to a clone of oneself!

What expectations do you have for your marriage and what expectations does your fiancé have? Are they realistic? Can they really be met? Bringing expectations into the open and examining them is necessary.

Unfulffilled Expectations

Unfulffilled expectations *generate frustration which leads to anger.* It is easy then for unfulfilled expectations to eventually *evolve into demands.* One spouse senses the demanding tone in the other's voice and is offended by it. To help define these expectations, try stating them in the form of a demand. Write them down. A husband's demands might be: "I demand that you get up first and cook my breakfast." "I demand that you always be home when I arrive after working all day." "I demand that you dress the way I've suggested in order to please me."

A wife's demands might be: "I demand that you work around

the house every Saturday." "I demand that you spend time with the children." "I demand that you become the spiritual leader in the home."

Dr. Joseph Maxwell describes the negative effects of such demands:

> Most of us are unaware of the demands we make on our spouse to exhibit certain traits or behaviors. What we are aware of is the feeling of anger or annoyance we experience when we are frustrated in realizing our demands. The feeling is so strong, so dependable, so apparently autonomous that we think it is not only justified but unavoidable. We believe that the feeling is caused by our spouse's failure rather than our demand. This occurs because we are very aware of the failure but are largely unaware of the demand which designates the failure as a bad event.
>
> Demandingness is a formidable barrier to marital growth because the person doing the demanding is likely to spend most of his or her time and energy catastrophizing and pitying self, and to spend little creative energy in planning ways to develop the relationship. Since every behavior of a spouse necessarily evokes a responsive behavior from the other spouse, such personally upsetting behavior as is produced by demandingness will usually have significant effects on the actions and feelings of the partner. In most cases, when one partner reacts negatively the other one responds by behaving equally negatively, creating an endless cycle of demandingness that leads away from growth and development of the relationship.
>
> If one spouse is willing to give up his or her demandingness, the cycle can not only be stopped, but reversed toward strengthening the marriage.[3]

What happens internally to a person whose demands are not met? The sequence flows something like this: A wife makes a demand of her husband but he does not meet it. She then becomes angry because she believes he "should" or "ought" to do what she demanded. (It is not he, but she who generates the anger.) Every time he fails to respond to the demand she says to herself, "It is awful." She then feels anger toward him and self-pity toward herself. Each time he fails to meet her demand, her emotional responses become more intense.

Changing Your Unfulfilled Expectations

When your expectations are unmet how will the problem be resolved? Of course one way is for your future spouse to give in and work harder to meet your needs. But this does not always happen, nor should it if your demand is unrealistic. Another solution that can greatly lessen the frustration and anger is for you to *change* your expectations of your future spouse.

To do this, first collect the list of those expectations of yours that have developed into demands. Then define and list the additional areas in which you have expectations. Now submit the demands and expectations to these questions:

1. Do we both have expectations in this area?
2. Do I have the same expectations of myself as I do of my fiancé? Why not?
3. How are our expectations of each other alike or different?
4. Whose expectations are stronger?
5. Whose expectations are most often met? Why? Because that person is older, stronger, more intelligent, male, more powerful?
6. Are my expectations more worthy of fulfillment than my fiancé's?
7. Where do my expectations originate? From parents, books, church, siblings, the neighborhood where I grew up?
8. Do all the people I know have the same expectations in a given area?
9. Do I have a "right" to my expectations?
10. Am I obligated to live up to my future spouse's expectations?

One way to reduce demands is to challenge them to see if they are rational or realistic. Ask yourself the following additional questions for each demand:

1. Is this expectation I have of my fiancé supported by objective reality? Is it objectively true that he or she should act this way?
2. Am I hurt in any way, shape or form if this expectation is not fulfilled?
3. Is this expectation essential to the attainment of any specific goal I have for my marriage?
4. What does this expectation do to my future spouse's perception of me?
5. Does this expectation help me achieve the kind of emotional responses I want for my spouse and me in marriage?

If you answered no to the first question and to at least two others, it is obvious that this expectation is invalid. If any demand or expectation is valid, then approach your fiancé in a new manner, such as: "I would appreciate it if you would . . . " or, "I would really prefer that you . . . . "

Another way you can evaluate your expectations of each other is to each list 20 of your expectations for your partner. Then write on a separate sheet of paper a two- or three-line paragraph about each expectation. The paragraph should explain how your own life and your marriage will be affected if that expectation is never met. Then exchange your lists of expectations, but not the paragraphs. Now each person has an opportunity to look at and to evaluate each expectation. You can respond to each expectation by making one of the following statements:

1. "I can meet this expectation most of the time and I appreciate knowing about this. Can you tell me why this is important to you?"
2. "I can meet this expectation some of the time and I appreciate knowing about this. Can you tell me why this is important to you? How can I share with you when I cannot meet this so it would be acceptable to you?"
3. "This expectation would be difficult for me to meet for these reasons. Can you tell me why this is so important

to you? How will this affect you? How can some adjustments be worked out?"

Here is a listing of one man's expectations. Those checked are the ones his fiancé was unsure about her ability to fulfill.

1. Personal daily Bible study—at least five days a week
2. I take care of finances (paying bills on time—not late); we get weekly allowances.
3. Faithful sexually
✓4. Exercise three times a week (½ hour each)✓
5. Own a dog and allow him to roam in living room (but not on the furniture)
6. Allow me to keep guns and not sell them
✓7. Equal participating in household chores (she assigned house cleaner once a week)✓
8. Have two or three children
9. She does not work while any of the children are under five and not in school
✓10. Never nag✓
11. Allow me to work out and go to exercise classes at least one day a week
12. Encourage me to study
13. Take the time to consider and listen to words and activities
14. Have summit meetings every three months
✓15. Spend one meal together daily if possible✓
16. We buy one major thing at a time
17. Credit cards are for *emergencies* only!
18. Nothing disturbs our meals together (phone off the hook)
✓19. My clothes mended within two weeks✓
✓20. Dishes done daily✓

Another area which is somewhat related to expectations has to do with the fears and concerns you may have about marriage. Since we hear so much about the potential struggles, we may enter marriage with fears. Have you identified your fears and discussed them with your fiancé? Often our fears tie in to some of our expectations. I ask couples in premarital counseling to identify their fears for me in the first session. If they cannot think of any I ask the question again in the next session. By the third session most couples have been able to identify them and we talk together in order to resolve them.

Here is a list of fears a 22-year-old woman brought to the third session of premarital counseling. Needless to say, our discussion was taken up for the entire time by these concerns. In fact, we also returned to them the next week. Note how they relate to expectations.

My Fears and Anxieties Entering Marriage

1. That we will be too busy to have quality time for each other
2. I will not be able to keep him and my mother happy— she will have her feelings hurt
3. His priority for working out and exercising will still be greater than mine
4. We will not have devotions or prayer together *every* day
5. There will be times when I will want to go into debt for a particular item and he will not
6. After a few years of marriage I will not want to give in and will want to "have it out"
7. I will want to concentrate on my career when he would rather begin having a family
8. I may want to decorate the house a little more formal than casual
9. I'll want to buy a new car—he'll want to buy a used one
10. I will get pregnant before we plan to

Setting Goals

Understanding your expectations will help you greatly as you begin to set goals for your marriage. Why are goals important?

The Value in Goal Setting

A goal is something we would like to achieve or see happen. It is a statement involving faith, for it tells of something we hope will happen in the future. "Faith is the substance of things hoped for" (Heb. 11:1, *KJV*). We all have goals, dreams or objectives and we proceed through life responding to these goals. How we are living is determined by the goal toward which we are working. Clearly defined goals give clarity to life, whereas muddled, hazy, unclear goals lead to confusion, purposelessness and depression. "Where there is no vision the people run wild" (Prov. 29:18, *Berkeley*).

Our goals motivate us toward the future. But what are our goals built upon—our own needs, wants and dreams or our spouse's or parents' needs, wants and dreams?

At this stage of your life you have probably attained numerous goals. Take time now to evaluate what you have accomplished so far in life.

1. List five goals that you have personally achieved in the past 10 years. Also indicate what you did to accomplish these goals.

Goals　　　　　　　　　　Steps I Took to Reach Them

1.　　　　　　　　　　　　1.

2.　　　　　　　　　　　　2.

3.　　　　　　　　　　　　3.

4.　　　　　　　　　　　　4.

5.　　　　　　　　　　　　5.

2. What has been accomplished in your relationship with your fiancé during the time you've been dating?

3. Are you satisfied with these accomplishments? If so, what other goals would you like to accomplish?

4. What specifically will you get out of marriage that you would not get if you remained single?

5. How much time will you spend each week enhancing or enriching your marriage?

6. What amount of money do you plan to set aside for marital enrichment each month?

The importance of goals has been stressed by psychiatrist Ari Kiev of the Cornell Medical Center:

> With goals people can overcome confusion and conflict over incompatible values, contradictory desires and frustrated relationships with friends and relatives, all of which often result from the absence of rational life strategies.
>
> Observing the lives of people who have mastered adversity, I have repeatedly noted that they have established goals and, irrespective of obstacles, sought with all their effort to achieve them. From the moment they've fixed an objective in their mind and decide to concentrate all their energies on a specific goal, they begin to surmount the most difficult odds.[4]

Goals give you a sense of direction. They are not what *will* be, but what you hope to attain. Because they are future oriented they can lift you from some of the difficulties of your present situation. Your focus can be upon positive hopes to come. As Christians we live in the present and future. Scripture admonishes us to have purposes and direction for our lives: "Forgetting the past and looking forward to what lies ahead, I strain to reach the end of the race" (Phil. 3:13-14, *TLB*); "A man's mind plans his way, but the Lord directs his steps" (Prov. 16:9, *RSV*). Once we set goals, our steps can be directed by the Lord.

Goals will help you use your time more effectively, for they help you sort out what is important and what is not. If you know what you intend or need to do, it is much easier to keep from being sidetracked.

I have a list of demands placed upon my time for ministry to others. Some time ago I determined how much time I have available for my speaking ministry each month, what I feel needs to be accomplished during these times of ministry and how best to accomplish the objectives. It is far easier now to evaluate requests and to say no to those that could detract me from the original God-directed goal.

Distinguishing Goals from Purposes

As we decide upon goals, we need to realize that a goal is an event in the future that is accomplishable and measurable. If I say that I want to be a good swimmer, I am stating a purpose. If I say that I want to be able to swim six laps in an Olympic-size pool by July 1, I am stating a goal.

Here are the characteristics of well-stated goals:

1. *A goal should be stated in terms of the end result.* Example: Spend two hours a week in direct, face-to-face communication with my wife.

2. *A goal should be achievable in a definite time period.* Example: Spend two hours a week in direct, face-to-face communication with my wife *by the end of February.*

3. *A goal should be definite as to what is expected.* Example:

Spend two hours a week in *direct, face-to-face communication* with my wife by the end of February.

4. *A goal should be practical and feasible.* Example: Spend *two hours* a week in direct, face-to-face communication with my wife by the end of February.

5. *A goal should be stated precisely in terms of quantities where applicable.* Example: Spend *two hours a week* in direct face-to-face communication with my wife by February.

6. *A goal should have one important goal or statement* rather than several.

Here is a list of goals written by a young woman in premarital counseling. She had been asked to select goals for her marriage. She was also asked to select a goal for her own life that she would like to achieve within three years and a goal for her fiancé to achieve within three years.

By Three Months

☐ 1. Make the first four minutes together each day (morning, evening, etc.) a quality time of building, affirming and affection.

☐ 2. Pray together daily (intercession, praise—more than just for meals); pray together on our knees in a 10- to 15-minute session once a week.

☐ 3. Study the Bible together once a week in addition to individual quiet times and/or reading Scripture at supper.

By Six Months

☐ 4. Refine communication patterns so that we go to sleep only after each partner is satisfied that he/she is understood and accepted by the other and that all is forgiven.

☐ 5. Practice hospitality—have children, another couple or a friend over for a meal twice a month.

☐ 6. Have feedback once a month on how marriage is going. Take 2- to 3-hour blocks and discuss growth and satisfactions as well as dissatisfactions and "unimportant things."

By One Year

☐ 7. Improve sexual patterns—creative, satisfying and exciting to both partners most of the time; understanding partner's moods, etc.

☐ 8. Be able to draw out the best in each of us; seek constructive criticism from each other and be able to give it.

Three-Year Goal for Him—Self-Image

☐ To see himself as worthy, having much to offer the psychological, evangelical, and his interpersonal worlds (i.e., not get depressed) regardless of accomplishments.

Three-Year Goal for Me—Flexibility

☐ To be flexible—able to take the other side, back down and admit I'm wrong in an argument; to be tolerant of other's views; to enjoy spontaneous guests for dinner or being a spontaneous guest for dinner.

Are the six characteristics of well-stated goals evident in this young woman's goals? In the squares before each of her goals, indicate which one(s) of the six characteristics are included. Use the numbers 1 through 6.

Developing Plans

Goal setting and priority-evaluation are not all of the process, however. Developing your plan to attain the goal is the heart of the process. Planning moves you from the present to the future.

You must be flexible and adaptable, because plans do change. Locking yourself into a dead-end approach would be as detrimental to your marriage as no goal-setting at all. This fact is stated in the book of Proverbs: "It is pleasant to see plans develop. That is why fools refuse to give them up even when they are wrong" (13:19, *TLB*). Planning is a tool, a means to an end. It saves time and energy and decreases frustration.

One husband described how he and his wife learned to plan their goals: "Before we were married, Evie's and my goals were just to get married. In the beginning years of our marriage, our major goals centered around my finishing seminary and getting into ministry. There were no goals for our life together as a couple except to be happy. Our first real mutual goal was to have a baby. It took us quite some time to realize that goal. Then it wasn't until we were in a seminar—a Christian Marriage Enrichment Seminar—about six years into our marriage that we thought about making mutual goals. This involved deciding upon them together and making them priorities in our lives.

"The experience in the seminar of setting mutual goals and then within the next few months working to reach some of those goals was so beneficial to our marriage that we decided to keep setting and reviewing goals periodically. So we began to set aside a couple of days between two and four times a year to do this. They became what we like to call 'honeymoon weekends.' They may not be on a weekend. We sometimes go away on a Tuesday and Wednesday or Thursday and Friday. The principle is that we get away from our regular routine and demands on our time and we go someplace where we can spend sufficient time together.

"We start on the first afternoon and evening by discussing goals that we previously set and evaluating the progress we've made. We also discuss setbacks and what adjustments we might need to make to reach the goals. We review the goals. About some goals we have made previously, we say, 'Well, that is not realistic,' or 'That is not practical,' or 'That is not so much a priority now as it was when we talked about it last time.'

"Then we spend some time on the second day of our honeymoon weekend talking about goals that involve others. We talk about where we would like to be in five years as a couple and as parents, as ministers, as people in our neighborhood—trying to take into account all aspects of life, including our relationship with God. Then we talk about what we would like to be doing a year from the present time in order to be on our way toward these five-year goals. We then talk about what needs to be done now to get started."

What can you do now to discover and set your goals? Ed Dayton and Ted Engstrom, in their book *Strategy for Living*, have given steps to setting goals. Respond to each of the following steps in the space provided. (You may want to review the difference between a goal and a purpose at this time.)

Step 1: Understand your purpose. What is it that you would like to do or your marriage to become? What is the general direction toward which you would like your marriage to move? Make a statement about that.

Step 2: Picture the situation. Imagine the situation of your marriage not as it is now, but as you would like it to be. What does it look like? Who are you with? What are you doing? What are the circumstances? Visualize and use your mental imagery.

Step 3: State some long-range goals. What measurable and accomplishable events would have to happen in order for that purpose to be realized?

Step 4: State your immediate goals. What are the things that you have to accomplish now if you are going to move toward your ultimate purpose in your marriage?

Step 5: Act. Pick out one of the goals for your marriage and start moving toward it. Remember that every long journey begins with the first step!

Step 6: Act as if . . . . Act as if you have already reached your goal. If you are going to start working toward that first goal, you are going to have to start acting as if you had really reached it. How would this impact on all the other parts of your life? What would it say about your plans for the church, your family, others? This may help you uncover some other goals that you need to consider.

Step 7: Keep praying. If you are going to live life with a purpose, then you need to keep seeking God's leading in all this. Yes, you have been praying through the whole planning process.

But pray, as well, before you act. If you are expecting to live a life with God's purpose in mind, you had better be communicating with Him.[5]

What do you want your marriage to reflect? Now is the time for you as an individual to begin setting some goals for your marital relationship. Using the information in this chapter, develop eight goals for your marriage. Here are a few ideas that may help you: "I want my marriage to reflect goals in finances, time spent together, recreation, roles and responsibilities, home life, ministry to other couples, sex life." "Our marriage should have goals for prayer and Bible study together, location and times of vacation, quantity of communication, trust in our relationship, etc."

7
COMMITMENT TO MAKE WISE DECISIONS

All couples develop a style of making decisions. Some styles are effective; some are self-defeating. How you will make decisions in your marriage determines whether this area of your marriage is strong and supportive or is weak and contributing to an eventual deterioration of your marriage.

Evaluating Your Decision-Making

For many couples decision-making is one of the most unenjoyable and even painful aspects of marriage. A couple who has never developed skills for competent decision-making suffers the consequences. They are less effective in coping with problem situations than couples who have developed mutually agreeable decision-making methods. They experience frustration, anger and stress. They feel unloved and end up being more dependent on others.

To determine where you now stand in the practice of decision-making, answer the following questions:

1. Who makes most of the decisions now, you or your fiancé? Why? How was this arrangement reached?

2. What guidelines have you developed to distinguish between a "minor" and a "major" decision once you are married?

3. What course of action will you follow when you disagree on a decision? Who will cast the deciding vote and why?

4. How have you decided which of the household chores each of you will perform?

5. Will you make any decisions without consulting your spouse? Which ones? How will this be decided?

6. Do you make decisions that you want to make or do you feel forced to decide in areas where you are uncomfortable? Which areas?

7. When are you most dominant in your relationship? When is your fiancé most dominant?

8. What guidelines do the Scriptures give concerning which decisions to make?

The Importance of Roles

In the book *The Mirages of Marriage,* Don Jackson and Richard Lederer state that the failure of couples to identify, determine and mutually assign areas of competence and responsibility, and determine who is in charge of what, is among the most destructive omissions in marriage.[1]

Certain tasks may appear quite clear-cut; many others are not. One myth that has been perpetuated over the years is that the husband *must* be in charge of certain areas and the wife *must* be in charge of others. It's like saying certain tasks are male and certain tasks are female. This thinking keeps many couples from being able to use their unique talents and gifts adequately to enrich their marriage. It is very difficult for many evangelical Christians to break away from this attitude.

If a person's temperaments, abilities and training are not suited to an established cultural role, he may become frustrated and question his abilities. He may also find devious means to avoid the responsibility and increasing conflict in his marriage. His spouse may question his abilities, too.

Even though we may not want or be able to fulfill the established cultural roles, our relationship requires order and an assignment of roles. Proverbs tells us: "The plans of the heart belong to man, but the answer of the tongue is from the Lord" (16:1, *NASB*). "Commit your works to the Lord, and your plans will be established" (16:3, *NASB*). "The plans of the diligent lead surely to advantage, but everyone who is hasty comes surely to poverty" (21:5, *NASB*). This does not mean that role assignments and guidelines are locked into the marriage forever. They must be open to frequent revision.

One of the common complaints about establishing a marriage

with a system of rules is that it is too rigid and unromantic. This system is thought to thwart the leading of the Holy Spirit in the relationship. Quite the contrary. Couples who overtly resist evaluating their marriage, setting goals and determining the area of decision-making and roles are usually threatened because they feel insecure and inadequate. They also may not have developed a life-style of self-discipline. They may have to make some changes.

When a couple has guidelines for making decisions, their behaviors are predictable. Predictability develops trust in their relationship, which in turn allows freedom to develop exceptions to the rules when necessary. Assigning both authority and responsibility creates flexibility in the relationship and thereby allows the couple to relax and give themselves to the tasks of enhancing their marriage and glorifying Christ.

What kind of trust do you want to develop as a couple? It is possible to develop negative trust as well as positive trust. If a spouse frequently does not live up to his promises or commitments, negative trust will develop. We can be predictable by not being trustworthy or dependable. This predictability, however, does not demonstrate love toward our partner. Spouses want the kind of predictability that creates positive trust.

Decision-Making Patterns

There are at least three basic decision-making patterns. One is the *stepwise* pattern, in which the decision is made according to a specified order. For example, a couple could agree to work on a problem, select one part to discuss, suggest possible solutions, and so on. All of the steps do not necessarily need to occur at the same time, but the process, once begun, is carried out in steps.

A second approach is the *non-stepwise* pattern. This simply means that all of the activities carried out in the process of making a decision do not occur in order. Certain portions of the process are omitted or even repeated.

A third type of decision-making is the *defaulted* pattern. In this pattern the decision is actually made for the other person and occurs as a result of either outside events or a lack of decision on the part of the other partner.

Identifying the Issues

Decision issues are not all the same. It is important to determine which *type* of decision issues are involved. The decision issues that occur regularly are labeled *recurring* issues. They can involve many different areas and often recur because of inadequate discussion and planning. Some of these might involve how much money to spend on clothing and food, how often to have the car serviced, use of time for recreation, etc.

Nonrecurring issues are those that come only occasionally or once in a lifetime. They could involve where to live, changing jobs, a child's college education, and the welfare of aging parents.

A *non-conjoint* issue is one in which both spouses are not needed to make a decision. There are several forms or subtypes of non-conjoint issues. One is the decision in which the outcome affects only one of the spouses—what to eat for lunch, what to wear, etc. Another subtype is the "factual" solution, where the outside evidence of facts actually decides the outcome for you. For example, if you want to purchase a new house, you may evaluate cost, interest, present savings and income. You may then discover that purchasing the house is just not possible for you at this time. It is your decision but it is based on the input of other persons or situations. Still another subtype of a non-conjoint issue requires expert opinion. This kind of decision-making usually involves medical, religious, technical or legal matters.

Perhaps you have never thought of the details of marital and family decisions like this. Many couples keep going on and on without any serious reflection about the types or styles of decisions, but close consideration may truly enhance and improve the relationship.

When we are making decisions, we encounter roadblocks. One roadblock is disagreeing on goals. When you disagree on goals, reaching a decision is difficult. Often couples don't know that their goals are different because they haven't talked about them!

...ions tend to be poor when you try to solve too many ...s at once. You may be eyeing one decision while still trying to make another. You may tend to insert elements from the second problem into the first, which only leads to confusion.

Your Role in Decision-Making

Following is a decision-making guide to help you determine how much influence you have in the decision-making process. Follow the instructions carefully.

Describe the decision-making process that you think you will have in your marriage by indicating the percentage of influence you will have and the percentage your spouse will have for each issue. The total for each decision must be 100 percent.

	Percentage of my vote	Percentage of my spouse's vote	Who I feel is more qualified to contribute to this decision. (Write your initial or your spouse's.
New car	_____	_____	_____
Home	_____	_____	_____
Furniture	_____	_____	_____
Your wardrobe	_____	_____	_____
Spouse's wardrobe	_____	_____	_____
Vacation spots	_____	_____	_____
Decor for the home	_____	_____	_____
Mutual friends	_____	_____	_____
Entertainment	_____	_____	_____
Church	_____	_____	_____
Child-rearing practices	_____	_____	_____
TV shows	_____	_____	_____

Home menu	_____	_____	_____
Number of children	_____	_____	_____
Where you live	_____	_____	_____
Husband's vocation	_____	_____	_____
Wife's vocation	_____	_____	_____
How money is spent	_____	_____	_____
How often to have sex	_____	_____	_____
Where to have sex	_____	_____	_____
Mealtimes	_____	_____	_____
Landscaping	_____	_____	_____
Various household tasks	_____	_____	_____

After each of you has completed this exercise, discuss it together.

It is commonly assumed that when a marriage contains a dominant spouse and a submissive spouse, the dominant one is the controlling one—in other words, the decision-maker. But in reality, the dominant one could be ineffective because the submissive one probably controls the relationship through passive resistance, such as withdrawing, being silent and refusing to give an opinion.

Let's consider another factor about decision-making. Which of you makes the decision more quickly? What effect does this have? In any relationship it is normal for one to be quicker and more decisive. This doesn't mean that the faster person is any more intelligent than the slower person.

The quicker spouse inserts his thoughts, plans and procedures into the discussion first and has a strong influence. He has the advantage and thus the slower person tends to become even slower. He can't keep pace or catch up.

In a marriage relationship it is usual for one to be quicker and more decisive than the other, and in the majority of cases the quicker decision-maker is at an advantage and his direction is usually adopted. The effect that this has on the slower person is that he tends to become slower and eventually give up. Why try? Thus he usually saves his response or reaction until the decision is made and then either shares approval or objections without having shared his thinking or reasoning on the matter.[2]

Father Chuck Gallagher suggests:

We can influence the other person to make a decision by our rate of speed. For example, a fast person may come up with one solution after another and force the other person to take one or another of what is offered. The slower one may initially turn down all of them, but after a while feel that he has been too negative by saying no, no, no. So he says yes just because so many solutions are presented.

On the other hand, a slow person can also exert pressure. He can give the impression that he is reliable, thoughtful and more to be trusted in making decisions, thus implying that the other person is rash or inexact. The ponderous person can be so slow-moving—examining every little detail—that he frustrates the other party to pieces.

A slow person can even put the blame on the partner when things go wrong and say, "Because you rushed so, you made me come to a decision when I wasn't ready for it—I didn't have time to think it through."

It is better that there be a commitment by both spouses to get involved in the overall decision-making process. We have to develop a "couple-pace" of making decisions rather than maintaining our individual paces. The slow person can learn to go a bit faster, and the faster one can learn to slow down. The point is to formulate our decisions together.

Of course, we may differ in other ways in our decision-making. One of us may be sharp, clear, definitive and decisive. The other one might be cautious, gentle, investigative, option-oriented. Each of these qualities is good and has definite advantages. But if we maintain our individual qualities and don't mesh ours with our spouse's, everything imaginable can occur.[3]

Looking Ahead

Where do we go from here in our decision-making? Consider these questions as a plan for evaluation and implementation:

If you and your fiancé could show a film of your parents' marital style, would you see your marriage reflected there? Will the responsibilities and control in your marriage be divided on the basis of traditional role expectations or upon what your own parents did? Traditional role structures are rigid in some cases, but some find definite security within the system. However, when one partner begins to ask, "Why do we do it this way?" or when children grow up and leave, problems may emerge. When a couple's life-style changes, the process of decision-making and role responsibilities change. Should the husband be the one to wash the car, mow the lawn, fix the roof? Should the wife be the one to cook, do the housework and care for the children? There may be more creative ways of functioning than following the traditional roles.

Is the responsibility for making decisions based on your abilities and giftedness? Does the control shift back and forth from one to another? If so, you probably will have a very efficient marriage in which each partner can be creative and grow as an individual.

Louis and Colleen Evans suggest cultivating spiritual gifts into the arena of roles and decision-making:

One of the first steps in putting gifts of the Spirit to

work in a marriage is to *believe* in such a thesis and to enter into the process of becoming aware, sensitive, and on the lookout for indications of your own and others' gifts.

Not all men are gifted in financial management; sometimes the wives are. In many mature and happy Christian homes we have seen the wife take the initiative in financial matters. True, there was always discussion about the decisions, and in the great majority of the circumstances, there was agreement. But in each, there was a quiet acceptance of her gift and an acquiescence to her counsel even though the "man was the head of the house."

Some men are not gifted in teaching; to require them to be the spiritual teacher as "head of the family" would be to put a heavy burden on their backs as well as create an atmosphere of awkwardness in the process, which repels rather than attracts the student. That does not mean a man might not "teach" in his own style of actions and responses to life's situations.

If the wife's gift is discovered to be something that takes her outside the home, then she and her husband need to consider the place of the children in their marriage. If they feel children are right for them then they ought to set aside the time to do the job right without feeling "hemmed in" or becoming victims of "cabin fever." The mature woman will not feel pushed out of shape or frustrated in the role of childbearing; she will be able to give herself to this process with joy and delight, for this is a phase of her life. If she cannot raise children in this attitude, then for God's sake and the child's sake she shouldn't have children; no one wants to feel unwanted or that he or she is an inconvenience. But so many, not wanting to "make the sacrifice," are yet pressured by the "standard role" and have children, resisting all the way.[4]

In this relationship it is important that each person be aware of what the other is thinking and the direction in which he is growing, so they can discuss issues knowledgeably. One caution, however; if you have specific areas of responsibility and decision-making for each of you, be sure to be as informed as possible concerning the other areas. Some couples have developed an isolation from each other because they divided their responsibilities to an extreme and failed to share them. Direct involvement and communication will eliminate this potential problem.

After you are married, you will need to ask yourself these questions:

Does one spouse fail to assume responsibility for making decisions, thus forcing the other to make the decision? Some couples do not make decisions but allow them to happen. This has been called decision by default. Usually the one who is affected least by the decision allows the other to make it. This approach is not always satisfactory. As long as one partner takes the abdicated responsibility, he reinforces the apathy of the other. It might be best not to take the responsibility so readily but to discuss the matter fully.

Too many husbands turn the responsibility for child-rearing decisions over to their wives, but the Scriptures indicate that the father is to be involved with the child. Note the following verses describing the father's task:

To chasten—Proverbs 19:18

To correct—Proverbs 22:15; 23:13

To teach—Deuteronomy 6:7; 11:18-21; Proverbs 1:8; 4:1-4

To nurture—Ephesians 6:4

Not to provoke to anger—Colossians 3:21

To provide for—1 Timothy 5:8; 2 Corinthians 12:14

To encourage—1 Thessalonians 2:11

To command—Genesis 18:19

To guide—Jeremiah 3:4

To discipline—Proverbs 3:12; Hebrews 12:5-7

Have you discussed together your methods for making decisions? What are the reasons behind the methods?

Sit down together during a time when no major decision

must be made and work out the process that you will follow. List three suggestions that you could offer to your spouse to help in the decision-making process.

Many couples develop a special, agreed-upon decision time when issues can be discussed, one at a time, with no interruptions. Try to carry the decision issue to the point of conclusion.

Will your plans for decision-making be successful? If you and your spouse begin to use one method of making decisions and it does not work well, experiment with another method. Different approaches need to be tried.

Have you ever asked your spouse if he/she has difficulty making decisions? Is it easy for him/her? Which areas are easy and which are difficult? Does he/she know whether it is difficult for you or easy for you? You cannot always judge by your spouse's outward behavior. He/she may be experiencing some inner conflict and may welcome input from you.

Have you agreed to make decisions in certain areas on your own without interference from your spouse? Many couples have numerous areas in which one is responsible for making decisions on his/her own. Some couples put a dollar limit on household or hobby items and do not have to consult the other unless the price exceeds the limit. One man stated in one of our marriage enrichment seminars that in the last 10 years he had not purchased one new item of clothing for himself. His wife buys everything and he is very satisfied with this arrangement. He hates to shop and he trusts her judgment. One couple stated that when they purchase a car that she will drive, she is primarily responsible for the choice. When it is for him, he has more to say.

What are some of the major decisions that each of you makes? What are the minor ones? Who will decide which are minor and which are major? How do you feel about these decisions? Is there an area in which you would like some assistance from your spouse or one in which you would like a greater voice? Some couples have written job division lists and then considered who has the time, ability and expertise to get the job done. They consider who is more concerned with each area and who enjoys the task the most.[5]

[It is] essential to realize that the spouse who *makes* the decisions is not necessarily the spouse who *controls* them. The key question ultimately is, "Who *decides* who decides?"

Husbands or wives often "delegate" decision areas to their partners so that while the actual decision is made by one, there is no doubt that the other holds the power. As we have pointed out, sometimes the "weaker" partner may actually have his or her mate jumping through hoops. A "helpless" husband may ask his wife to lay out his clothing every morning so that his socks, shoes, tie, shirt, and suit will coordinate. *She decides* what he will wear, but *he has decided* that she is to be his "valet." A "depressed" wife may have everyone in the household catering to her "bad" days. Many books and articles have been written telling wives how to fool husbands into believing they are "lords and masters" by appearing to defer to them on the surface. This game playing backfires in the long run. Finding the patterns you use to make decisions, altering them to suit your needs, and having a variety of decision-making methods to use for different circumstances are the realistic and effective techniques that make a marriage function well.[6]

Do our thoughts and decisions reflect our relationship with the Lord? The one person most often left out of the decision-making process is Jesus Christ. The lordship of Christ means His direction should be involved in our decisions. Colossians 3:17 *(NASB)* states: "And whatever you do in word or deed, do all in the name of the Lord Jesus, giving thanks through Him to God the Father."

We read in Ephesians 4:23 *(NASB)* that we are to "be renewed in the spirit of your mind." This passage speaks of God's Spirit influencing man's mental attitude. This should also include our reasons and motivations for our decisions.

One of the major questions usually asked has to do with the impasse. When each person is committed to his own point of view or belief, further negotiation seems unlikely to produce any change. James Jauncey, in his book *Magic in Marriage,* points out that the Christian husband and wife have specific help for everyday problems, not only from the guidelines in the Scriptures but also in the daily presence of the Holy Spirit. Jauncey says:

> God through His Holy Spirit seeks our best welfare and happiness. He seldom does this by a supernatural act. Instead, He seeks to permeate our thinking until our judgments are His.
>
> In marriage He has two people to work through. The husband's authority does not carry infallibility with it. Since the two become "one flesh" the guidance has to come through both. This means that except in cases of emergency, decision affecting the whole family should not be put into effect until they are unanimous.[7]

Look at the following time sequence. Indicate the major decisions you will need to make during the time periods indicated. These decisions may concern your personal life, vocation, children, other family members, vacations, etc.

Within the next five years:

Within the next 10 years:

Within the next 15 years:

Within the next 20 years:

Within the next 30 years:

Which of you will have the most to contribute concerning each decision? Why? In what way will the Word of God help you in these decisions?

8
COMMITMENT TO COMMUNICATION

Defining Communication

If you came to me for premarital counseling and asked, "What is the most important issue of marriage that we need to be aware of?" I would say, "Communication!" Above all else you will need to learn to communicate in a way that will build your relationship and bring glory to God. Without communication there is no relationship. This is true right now in your relationship with your fiancé and with God. Reuel Howe said, "Communication is to love what blood is to the body."[1] Take the blood out of the body and it dies. Take communication away and a relationship dies. Howe also said, "If there is any indispensable insight with which a young married couple should begin their life together, it is that they should try to keep open, at all cost, the lines of communication between them."[2]

Communication is both talking and silence; it is touching and a quiet look.

Communication is the process of sharing yourself both verbally and nonverbally in such a way that the other person can understand and accept what you are sharing. Of course, it means you also have to attend with your ears and eyes so that the other person can communicate with you.

Communication is accomplished only when the other person

receives the message you send, whether verbal or nonverbal. Communication can be effective, positive and constructive, or it can be ineffective, negative and destructive. While one spouse may intend the message to be positive, the other spouse may receive it as a negative.

The Word of God is the most effective resource for learning to communicate. In it you will find a workable pattern for healthy relationships. Here are just a few guidelines it offers:

- "But speaking the truth in love, we are to grow up in all aspects into Him, who is the head, even Christ" (Eph. 4:15, *NASB*).
- "A man who refuses to admit his mistakes can never be successful. But if he confesses and forsakes them, he gets another chance" (Prov. 28:13, *TLB*).
- "For we all stumble in many ways. If any one does not stumble in what he says, he is a perfect man, able to bridle the whole body as well" (Jas. 3:2, *NASB*).
- "Let him who means to love life and see good days refrain his tongue from evil and his lips from speaking guile (1 Pet. 3:10, *NASB*).
- "Some people like to make cutting remarks, but the words of the wise soothe and heal" (Prov. 12:18, *TLB*).
- "A wise man controls his temper. He knows that anger causes mistakes" (Prov. 14:29, *TLB*).
- "Gentle words cause life and health; griping brings discouragement . . . . Everyone enjoys giving good advice, and how wonderful it is to be able to say the right thing at the right time! (Prov. 15:4,23, *TLB*).
- "Timely advice is as lovely as golden apples in a silver basket" (Prov. 25:11, *TLB*).
- "A friendly discussion is as stimulating as the sparks that fly when iron strikes iron" (Prov. 27:17, *TLB*).
- "Pride leads to arguments; be humble, take advice and become wise" (Prov. 13:10, *TLB*).
- "Love forgets mistakes; nagging about them parts the best of friends" (Prov. 17:9, *TLB*).
- "Let all bitterness and wrath and anger and clamor and slander be put away from you, along with all malice. And be kind

to one another, tender-hearted, forgiving each other, just as God in Christ also has forgiven you" (Eph. 4:31-32, *NASB*).

Communication that is effective depends not so much on what is said but on why and how it is shared. Much of the conversation between married couples is simply conveying information—"I had a rough day at work today"—which is really the least important purpose of marital communication.

Why do we seek to really communicate with one another? For some of us it is a way of achieving empathy with our spouse. We want to know that our partner feels what we are feeling. We want someone to share our positive feelings and our joys, as well as our negative feelings and sorrow. Romans 12:15 exhorts us to do this.

Sometimes, rather than merely conveying information, we desire to draw the other person into our life. When we are encouraged to talk about what happened to us at work, at home or at church, we feel accepted by our spouse.

Another reason for sharing is to ventilate anger and pain. Not only do we need to express our emotions, we also need someone to listen and accept us. We need a sounding board; however, our listener needs inner security and emotional stability in order to be a sounding board.

The foregoing are a few of the reasons why we share with one another, but they all boil down to one basic need—we want to be affirmed and supported by the person we love. This kind of support reinforces our own beliefs or feelings about ourselves. We need positive (not negative) feedback that says, "You are adequate, lovable, good, nice to be around, etc." Marcia Lasswell and Norman Lobenz in their outstanding book *No-Fault Marriage* suggest four levels of support:

Support Level 1 is what we all desire. This is when you are in total agreement with your partner's goals, ideas or beliefs. Many people feel this is the only type of support that has any value. It is the easiest to give because supporting what you agree with does not make an overwhelming demand on your love or concern.

Support Level 2 is when you do not agree with what your fiancé or spouse wants to do, but you will provide support to whatever extent you can. This support is based upon respect for your partner.

Support Level 3 is sort of a hands-off position. You disagree with your fiancé or spouse and cannot give any kind of support. But you do not create problems or obstacles for him/her.

Support Level 4 is really *no* support. Not only do you disagree with your fiancé or spouse but you attempt to prevent him/her from doing what he/she wants to do.

1. Give an example of a time when you experienced each support level and tell how you felt.
   Support Level 1:

   Support Level 2:

   Support Level 3:

   Support Level 4:

2. In what area of your life would you like Level 1 support from your fiancé?

3. How could you express this particular concern to your fiancé?

4. In what area of his/her life would your fiancé like Level 1 support from you?

What Do Your Words Mean?

When a couple marries, two distinct cultures and languages come together. In fact, you are actually marrying a foreigner. Surprised? You may be! But each of you speaks a different language with different meanings to the same words. If each of you does not define your words, then assumptions and misunderstandings will occur. A husband tells his wife that he will be home early tonight. What is his definition of "early"? What is his wife's definition? Or when a wife responds to her husband's request, "I'll do it later," what does that loaded word "later"

mean? The wife may mean, "I'll do it in three days." Her husband may interpret it as, "She'll do it in three hours."

Nonspecific commitments such as, "I'll think about it," create disagreements and frustration. The response, "Yes, I'll try," is also insufficient. Nothing may happen but the spouse can still say, "But I'm trying." A definite and specific commitment is more acceptable.

"I will call you if I see that I will be late for dinner."

"I will help clean up the family room starting this Saturday."

"I will help you in disciplining John by . . . "

"I will have dinner ready by the time you arrive home from the office."

"I will begin praying with you and we will pray together at least three days a week."

A significant question for couples to ask each other is, "To what extent do we both mean the same thing by the words we use?" Two people can speak Spanish and not mean the same thing. Two people can speak German and not mean the same thing. Two people can speak English and not mean the same thing. Our own experience, mind-set and intent give meaning to our words. Have you ever experienced one of the following situations?

"Could I talk to you for a minute?" your fiancé asks. You say yes, assuming he/she means "a minute." Forty minutes later your fiancé is still talking and you are becoming agitated and restless.

"Could you please pick up one or two things at the market for me?" your fiancé asks. After you agree you discover that "one or two things" involves four different stops at locations scattered away from your main route to see your fiancé and you end up late for your evening with him/her.

You and your fiancé are on your way to a football game and he/she asks, "Could we stop at the store just for a minute? I need one item." Thirty minutes later you are still waiting in the car.

Even when we raise our voices when we communicate means something different to each person. Yelling may be a normal form of expression for one person, whereas to the other it means anger and being out of control.

A husband responds to his wife's question of "How did you like the dinner?" with "Fine." To him the word means "Great, very satisfying. I liked it a lot." But to his wife it means he had little interest in what he was eating. If the situation was reversed she would use several sentences and lots of adjectives to describe her delight. He uses a single word. But both people may mean the very same thing.

One of the most vicious and destructive communication techniques is silence. It can be devastating. Each of us needs to be recognized and acknowledged. But when our partner retreats into silence our very presence, existence and significance are ignored by the most significant person in our lives. In fact, many people would consider such silence an insult!

Silence can communicate a multitude of things: happiness, satisfaction, a sense of contentment and well-being. But more often than not it communicates dissatisfaction, contempt, anger, pouting, sulking, "who cares," "who gives a darn," "I'll show you," etc. When silence prevails there is little opportunity to resolve issues and move forward in a relationship. "Talk to me," we beg and our fiancé gets angry or continues to withdraw through silence. Too many of us use silence as a weapon.

But think about the meaning of silence for a moment. What is silence? It is really a form of communication and if we respond accordingly we may get our fiancé to open up. "What do you think about the question I've asked you?" you might say. Or, "Your silence is telling me something. I wonder what you're trying to communicate to me through it?" or "I'd like to talk to you about your silence and what it does to me. But first I'd like to hear what you think about your silence."

Another approach might be, "I've noticed that there are times when it's difficult for you to talk to me. Is there something I'm doing that makes it so difficult for you to share with me that you'd rather be silent?" If your fiancé responds with an answer to this, just let him/her talk. Do not attempt to defend yourself. Thank him/her for sharing his/her feelings with you. If he/she has not told you what it is that he/she wants you to do differently, ask him/her for a suggestion.

What Do Your Nonverbals Say?

We sing, we cry, we talk, we groan, we make simple or extended sounds of happiness, joy, despair or anger. This is verbal communication. We touch, gesture, withdraw, frown, slam doors, look at another person. These are forms of nonverbal communication.

Are you aware of the effect your nonverbal communication has upon your fiancé? We use gestures, body movements and eye expressions constantly, but often our awareness of them is minimal. Frequently our words convey a message of approval or permission, but our nonverbals express a conflicting message of disapproval. This means the listener *hears* approval and *sees* disapproval. The result is confusion. Often the listener ignores the spoken message and responds to the nonverbal. Or if he does respond to the words, the speaker becomes irritated and the listener wonders why the speaker is upset.

Body movements provide a basis for making some reasonable assumptions but not for drawing absolute conclusions. It is important, therefore, that couples learn to do the following:

1. Become aware of the nonverbal messages you send your fiancé.
2. Become skillful in correctly interpreting the nonverbals which your fiancé sends you.
3. Develop a fluency in your nonverbal skills.
4. Learn how to bring your nonverbal communication and your spoken communication into harmony.

Nonverbal communication is similar to a code. We need to learn to decipher it, modify, refine and enhance it. Tone of voice and inflection add another element to the communication process. The mixture can be rather complicated.

Three Components of Communication

Every message has three components: (1) the actual content, (2) the tone of voice, and (3) the nonverbal communication. It is possible to express many different messages using the same word, statement or question simply by changing your tone of voice or body movement. Nonverbal communication includes facial expression, body posture and actions.

The three components of communication must be complementary in order for a simple message to be transmitted. One researcher has suggested that successful communication consists of 7 percent content, 38 percent tone of voice, 55 percent nonverbal communication.

We often send confusing messages because the three components are contradicting each other. When a man says to his wife with the proper tone of voice, "Dear, I love you," but with his head buried in a newspaper, what is she to believe? When a woman asks, "How was your day?" in a flat tone while passing her husband on the way to the other room, what does he respond to, the verbal or the nonverbal message?

A husband, as he leaves for work comes up to his wife, smiles, gives her a hug and a kiss and states in a loving voice, "I really love you." After he leaves she feels good. But when she notices the newspaper in the middle of the room, pajamas on the bed, dirty socks on the floor and the toothpaste tube with the cap off lying in the sink, her good feeling begins to dissipate. She has told her husband how important it is to her that he assume responsibility for cleaning up after himself because it makes extra work for her when he doesn't. But he has been careless again. She believed him when he left for work, but now she wonders, "If he really meant what he said and really loves me, why doesn't he show it by assuming some responsibility? I wonder if he really does love me." His earlier actions contradicted his message of love, even though the message may have been sent properly.

Concerning communication, Dr. Mark Lee writes:

> Marital problems may grow out of unsatisfactory nonverbal communications. Vocal variables are important carriers of meaning. We interpret the sound of a voice, both consciously and subconsciously. We usually can tell the emotional meanings of the speaker by voice pitch, rate of speech, loudness, and voice quality. We can tell

the sincerity or the insincerity, the conviction or the lack of conviction, the truth or the falsity of most statements we hear. When a voice is raised in volume and pitch, the words will not convey the same meaning as when spoken softly in a lower register. The high, loud voice, with rapid rate and harsh quality, will likely communicate a degree of emotion that will greatly obscure the verbal message. The nonverbal manner in which a message is delivered is registered most readily by the listener. It may or may not be remembered for recall. However, the communicator tends to recall what he said rather than the manner of his speech.[3]

Are You Visual, Auditory or Feeling?

Communication means different things to different people. In counseling it soon becomes apparent that married couples who are having "communication" problems have different communication styles. As I mentioned earlier in this chapter, when a couple marries, two different cultures and languages come together. For a relationship to blossom, each must learn the other's language. And each must be willing to use the other's language without demanding that the other person become like him/her.

When people communicate they process their information in different ways. Some people are more *visual,* some are more *auditory* and some are more *feeling* oriented. Some people think by generating visual images in their minds, some respond from the feeling level, others talk to themselves and hear sounds (No, they aren't wacky!).

You may be primarily a visual person. You see the sentences that you speak in your mind. Another person responds best to what he hears. The feeling person has a heightened sense of touch and emotion or intuition. He responds on the basis of his feelings.

Each of us has a dominant mode of perception. We have been trained to function primarily in that mode. *But it is possible for a person to learn to function and communicate in the other modes as well*. What are you like? Are you primarily a visual, auditory or feeling person? What is your fiancé? Are you aware of your differences and similarities? Can you communicate or do you usually pass one another in the night?

An easy way to understand the way in which you and your fiancé communicate is to pay attention to the words, images and phrases you both use.

What do these phrases say to you?

"I *see* what you are saying."

"That *looks* like a good idea. *Show* me more about it."

"I would like to know your *point of view*."

"Let's *focus* in on just one subject."

These phrases reflect a visual bias. The person thinks and speaks on the basis of strong visual pictures. Other people see vague pictures and some no pictures at all.

"I *hear* you."

"Boy, that *sounds* great to me."

"*Tell* me that again."

"That's coming through *loud and clear*."

"Let's *hear* that again."

These phrases come from a person who is basically auditory. Sounds are of primary importance to him.

"I *sense* that you are upset with me."

"This shoe has a good *feel* to me."

"My *instincts* say this is the right thing to do."

These are phrases coming from a person who responds in a feeling mode. Perhaps you have been in a group where a new idea has been shared. If, at that time, you had been aware of these three modes of responding you may have heard, "That idea *feels* good," "That idea *looks* good," and "That *sounds* like a good idea." They all mean the same thing but are presented via three different processes.

What does all this have to do with husband-wife communication? Just this! If each of you learn to use the other's style of speaking *(perceptual mode)* you will each listen better. It may be a bit of work and take you a while to become skillful at it but it can work. Too often one person expects the other to cater to him/her and do it his/her way. But if you are willing to take the initiative and move into his/her world first, then you establish a common ground for communication.

There are occasions when you may feel that your fiancé is resisting your idea or suggestion. It could be that you have failed to communicate in a way that he/she can understand. If you ask a question and do not receive the right response, switch to another way of asking the question. "How does this sound to you?" No response. "Does this look all right to you?" No response. "How do you feel about this issue?" A response!

A wife asks her husband to complete a chore. He responds by saying, "Write it down," or "Make me a list." If in the future she makes a list or note and gives it to him at the same time she tells him, she may get a quicker response.

Once you are able to communicate with your fiancé in his/her mode, your fiancé may be willing to move into your world. If you learn to see, hear and feel in the same way that your fiancé sees, hears and feels, communication is bound to improve. We all use all three modes, but one is better developed in each of us than the others.

I have found these principles essential when communicating with my clients in the counseling office. As I listen I try to discover their perceptual mode so that I can enter into their world with them. I listen also to their tone of voice and phrases. I study their nonverbals. Some couples are loud, expressive, gesture a lot, use many nonverbals. Others come in and are somewhat quiet, reserved, very proper and choose their words carefully. I need to communicate as they do first so that eventually they are willing to listen and move the direction I would like them to move.

Basically I am a visual person, but I have learned to use all three modes. I still prefer the visual, however. If someone brings me a letter or something he has written and says, "Listen to this," my first response is, "Oh, let me see it." I prefer reading it myself rather than listening to it being read. It registers more with me and I digest it more quickly. When I discover some new exciting material that I would like to share with my students, my first inclination is, "How can I diagram this and use it on charts and overhead transparencies so others can see it?" I am more conscious of my tendency to use visual words. But not everyone responds the way I do. Thus I need to broaden my responses to include the auditory and feeling modes. By doing this, others can understand me and I can better understand them as well—and so can you.

How to Develop Communication

What can you and your fiancé do to develop your communication?

1. Become more sensitive to the words and phrases others use. Listen to a friend or colleague, or listen to someone on TV or radio. Can you identify the person's perceptual mode?

2. Make a list of the various phrases you use during the day. What is your dominant mode?

3. Make a list of the various phrases your fiancé uses. What is his or her dominant mode? Practice using that style. You may need to expand your vocabulary so that you are better able to speak your fiancé's language. Unfortunately there is no Berlitz language course to teach you this new language. It is something you will have to teach yourself.[4]

These are just a few basic ideas about communication. Many of these I have been sharing with married couples in counseling and seminars. Many people have said, "I wish I had known about this when we were first married. It would have made such a difference." I hope it will make a difference for you. In the next two chapters we will continue to discuss communication by focusing on listening and communication guidelines.[5]

5. For a detailed Bible study on communication, complete chapter 9 of the book *Before You Say I Do* by Wes Roberts and H. Norman Wright, published by Harvest House Publishers.

9
COMMITMENT TO LISTEN

One of the greatest gifts one person can give to another is the gift of listening. It can be an act of love and caring. Too often conversations today between married couples are dialogues of the deaf. If a husband listens to his wife, she feels, "I must be worth hearing." If a wife ignores her husband, he thinks, "I must be dull and boring."

Have you had the experience of being really listened to? Look at these verses from the Word of God that talk about how God listens:

- "The eyes of the Lord are toward the righteous, and His ears are open to their cry. The face of the Lord is against evildoers, to cut off the memory of them from the earth. The righteous cry and the Lord hears, and delivers them out of all their troubles. The Lord is near to the brokenhearted, and saves those who are crushed in spirit" (Ps. 34:15-18, *NASB*).

- "I love the Lord, because He hears my voice and my supplications. Because He has inclined His ear to me, therefore I shall call upon Him as long as I live" (Ps. 116:1-2, *NASB*).

- "Call to Me, and I will answer you, and I will tell you great and mighty things, which you do not know" (Jer. 33:3, *NASB*).

The Word of God also gives us directives concerning how *we* are to listen:

- "He who gives an answer before he hears, it is folly and shame to him (Prov. 18:13, *NASB*).

- "Any story sounds true until someone tells the other side and sets the record straight" (Prov. 18:17, *TLB*).
- "The wise man learns by listening; the simpleton can learn only by seeing scorners punished" (Prov. 21:11, *TLB*).
- "Let every man be quick to hear (a ready listener)" (Jas. 1:19, *AMP*).

A Deffinition

What do we mean by listening? What do we mean by hearing? Is there a difference? Yes, there is. Hearing is basically to gain content or information for your own purposes. Listening is caring for and being empathic toward the person who is talking. Hearing means that you are concerned about what is going on inside *you* during the conversation. Listening means you are trying to understand the feelings of *the other person* and are listening for his sake.

Let me give you a threefold definition of listening. Listening means that when your fiancé is talking to you:

1. You are not thinking about what you are going to say when he/she stops talking. You are not busy formulating your response. You are concentrating on what is being said and are putting into practice Proverbs 18:13.

2. You are completely accepting what is being said without judging what he/she is saying or how he/she says it. You may fail to hear the message if you are thinking that you don't like your fiancé's tone of voice or the words he/she is using. You may react on the spot to the tone and content and miss the meaning. Perhaps he/she hasn't said it in the best way, but why not listen and then come back later when both of you are calm and discuss the proper wording and tone of voice? Acceptance does not mean you have to agree with the content of what is said. Rather, it means that you understand that what your fiancé is saying is something he/she feels.

3. You should be able to repeat what your fiancé has said and what you think he/she was feeling while speaking to you. Real listening implies an obvious interest in your fiancé's

feelings and opinions and an attempt to understand them from his/her perspective.

Failing to listen may actually increase the amount of talking coming your way as one writer explains:

> Your wife may be a compulsive talker. Was she always that way, even before you were married? Or did she just seem to get that way with time? Some women talk at the moment of birth and a steady stream follows each moment of their lives forever after, but others have developed a nonstop flow of talk for other reasons. Many times a compulsive talker is really shouting to be heard by someone. The more bored you look, the more you yawn, the more you watch the dog or TV, the harder she talks. She just talks all the more to compensate. You may have stopped listening a long time ago, and she knows that better than anybody.
>
> Do you think this has happened to you? When was the last time that you asked these questions of your wife? "How do you feel about . . . ?" Do you ever intersperse her remarks with, "You may be right, Hon." If your wife feels you are not willing to listen to her, she has two options: to talk louder and harder; or to talk less and withdraw. Either way, it's very hard on the marriage.[1]

You can learn to listen, for it is a skill to be learned. Your mind and ears can be taught to hear more clearly. Your eyes can be taught to see more clearly. But the reverse is also true. You can learn to *hear* with your *eyes* and *see* with your *ears*. Jesus said: "Therefore I speak to them in parables; because while seeing they do not see, and while hearing they do not hear, nor do they understand. And in their case the prophecy of Isaiah is being fulfilled, which says, 'You will keep on hearing, but will not understand; and you will keep on seeing, but will not perceive; for the heart of this people has become dull, and with their ears they scarcely hear, and they have closed their eyes lest they should see with their eyes, and hear with their ears, and under-

stand with their heart and turn again, and I should heal them'" (Matt. 13:13-15, *NASB*).

Let your ears hear and see.

Let your eyes see and hear.

The word *hear* in the New Testament does not usually refer to an auditory experience; it usually means "to pay heed." As you listen to your fiancé you need "to pay heed" to what he or she is sharing. It means tuning into the right frequency.

Because my retarded son, Matthew, does not have a vocabulary, I have learned to listen to him with my eyes. I can read his nonverbal signals which carry a message. Because of Matthew I have learned to listen to what my counselees cannot put into words. I have also learned to listen to the message behind the message—the hurt, the ache, the frustration, the loss of hope, the delight, the promise of change. I reflect upon what I see on a client's face, posture, walk, pace and tell him/her what I see. This gives him/her an opportunity to explain further what he/she is thinking and feeling. He/she *knows* I'm tuned to him/her.

There are many types of listening. Some people listen for facts, information and details for their own use. Others listen because they feel sorry for the person. They feel a sense of pity. Some people listen to gossip because they revel in the juicy story of another person's failures or difficulties. There are occasions when people listen out of obligation, necessity or to be polite. Some who listen are nothing more than voyeurs who have an incessant need to pry and probe into other people's lives.

Some listen because they care. Why do you listen? What are your motives? Any or all of the above? Listening that springs from caring builds closeness, reflects love and is an act of grace.

Sensitive listening and hearing are open mine shafts to intimacy. Too often the potential for listening lies untapped within us like a load of unmined gold. All of us have barriers that inhibit our listening. Some are simple and others complex.

Obstacles to Listening

In order for caring listening to occur we need to be aware of some of the common listening obstacles to communication.

Defensiveness is a common obstacle. You are busy in your mind thinking up a rebuttal, an excuse or an exception to what your fiancé is saying. In doing this you miss the message. There are a variety of defensive responses.

First, perhaps you reach a premature conclusion. "All right, I know just what you're going to say. We've been through this before and it's the same old thing."

Second, you may read into his/her words your own expectations or project what you would say in the same situation. David Augsburger writes, "Prejudging a communication as uninteresting or unimportant lifts the burden of listening off one's shoulders and frees the attention to wander elsewhere. But two persons are being cheated: the other is not being given a fair hearing and the listener is being deprived of what may be useful information. I want to cancel all advance judgments—prejudgments—and recognize them for what they are, prejudices. I want to hear the other in a fresh, new way with whatever energies I have available."[2]

Third, you may rehearse your responses. Rehearsing a response (as well as other defensive postures) is not what the Scripture is calling you to do as a listener. "He who answers a matter before he hears the facts, it is folly and shame to him" (Prov. 18:13, *AMP*).

Fourth, you may respond by using gun-power words. Gun-power words hook you into a negative defensive response. They create an inner explosion of emotions. Gun-power includes, "That's crude"; "That's just like a *woman* (or man)"; "You're *always* late"; "You *never* ask me what I think"; "You're becoming just like your mother." Not only do we react to gun-power words but we may consciously choose to use some, which makes it difficult for our fiancé to listen. What are the gun-power words that set you off? What is your fiancé's list of gun-power words? Certain selected words can cut and wound.

Not all defensiveness is expressed, however. Outwardly we could be agreeing but inside we are saying just the opposite. If your fiancé confronts you about a behavior or attitude you display that is creating a problem, do you accept the criticism or do you react in a defensive manner?

Look at the guidance of Scripture:

- "If you refuse criticism you will end in poverty and disgrace; if you accept criticism you are on the road to fame" (Prov. 13:18, *TLB*).
- "Don't refuse to accept criticism; get all the help you can" (Prov. 23:12, *TLB*).
- "It is a badge of honor to accept valid criticism" (Prov. 25:12, *TLB*).
- "A man who refuses to admit his mistakes can never be successful. But if he confesses and forsakes them, he gets another chance" (Prov. 28:13, *TLB*).

Another listening obstacle may be attitudes or biases you hold toward certain individuals. These could include people who speak in a certain tone of voice, ethnic groups, the opposite sex, people who remind us of someone from our past, etc. Because of our biases we reject the person or the personality without listening to what the person has to say. In effect we are saying, "If you're . . . (and I don't like people who are . . .) I don't need to listen to you."

Our own personal biases will affect how well we listen more than we realize. For example, it may be easier for us to listen to an angry person than a sarcastic person; some tones or phrases are enjoyable to listen to, whereas others may be annoying; repetitive phrases which another uses (and may be unaware of) can bother us; even excessive gestures such as talking with the hands or waving arms can be a distractor. Some people are distracted in their listening because of the sex of the person who is speaking. Our expectations of what a man shares or doesn't share and what a woman should or should not share will influence us.

We may listen more or less attentively to someone who is in a position over us, under us or in a prestigious position.

We may assign stereotypes to other people and this influences our listening to them.

One person hears with optimism and another with pessimism. I hear the bad news and you hear the good news. If your fiancé shares a frustration and difficult situation with you, you may not hear him because you don't like complaining; it bothers you. Or you may hear him as a person who trusts you enough to share.

Your own inner struggles may block your listening. We have difficulty listening when our emotional involvement reaches the point where we are unable to separate ourselves from the other person. You may find it easier to listen to the problems of other people rather than your own fiancé's because you are hindered by your emotional involvement. Listening may also be difficult if you blame yourself for the other person's difficulties.

Hearing what someone else is saying may bring to the surface feelings about similar problems you are facing. Your listening may be hindered if you are fearful that your own emotions may be activated too much. You may feel very ill at ease as your emotions begin to surge to the surface. Can you think of a time when in listening to another person you felt so overwhelmed with feelings that you were unable to hear?

If someone has certain expectations for you, you may be hindered in listening to that person. If you dislike the other person you probably will not listen to him very well. When people speak too loudly or softly you may struggle to keep listening.

Do you know what hinders your listening? Who is responsible for the obstacle? Your partner or you?

You can overcome the obstacles. The initial step is to identify the obstacle. Of those listed, which obstacle do you identify as yours? Who controls this barrier? You or the one speaking? Perhaps you can rearrange the situation or conditions so that listening would be easier. You may need to discuss as a couple what each of you can do to become a better listener and what you can do to make it easier for your fiancé to listen to you.

Another obstacle that hurts the listening process is similar to defensiveness—it is interrupting. You may erect this barrier because you feel the other person is not getting to the point fast enough. Or you may be thinking ahead and start asking for information that would be forthcoming anyway. Your mind wanders and races ahead. You say, "Hold it. I've got a dozen ideas cooking because of what you said. Let me tell you some of them . . . " It is easy for our minds to wander, for we think at five times the rate we speak. If a person speaks at 100 words a minute and you listen at 500, do you put your mind on hold or daydream the rest of the time? You process information faster than it can be verbalized, so you can choose to stay in pace with the speaker or let your mind wander.

You may find yourself facing yet another obstacle—overload. Perhaps you have used up all the space available in your mind for information. Someone else comes along with a new piece of information and you feel you just can't handle it. You feel as though you are being bombarded from all sides and you don't have enough time to digest it all. Thus it becomes difficult to listen to anything. Your mind feels like a juggler with too many items to juggle.

Timing is another common obstacle. Both mental and physical fatigue make it difficult to listen. There are times when you need to let your partner know that this is not a good time, but tell him/her when you *will* be able to listen.

Have you heard of selective attention? Another way of expressing this obstacle is *filtered listening,* screening the information being shared. If we have a negative attitude we may ignore, distort or reject positive messages. Often we hear what we want to hear or what fits in with our mind-set. If we engage in selective listening we probably engage in selective retention. That means we remember certain comments and situations and forget those we reject. David Augsburger describes the process this way:

> Memory is the greatest editor of all, and it discards major pieces of information while treasuring trifles. When I try to work through an unresolved conflict that is only an hour old, I find my memory—which I present as though it were complete, perfect and unretouched— is quite different from my partner's—which I can see is partial, biased and clearly rewritten. We both have selective memories.
>
> Selectivity is an asset. It saves us from being overloaded with stimuli, overwhelmed with information,

overtaxed with demands from a humming, buzzing environment.

Selectivity is also a liability. If I deny that it is taking place there will be much that I don't see, and I won't see that I don't see. If I pretend I saw it all, understood it all, recall it all, there will be many times when I will argue in vain or cause intense pain in relationship with my inability to hear the other whose point of view is equally good, although probably as partial as my own. We each—even at our best—see in part, understand only in part, and recall only a small part.[3]

Seven Steps to Better Listening

How can you become a better listener?

Understand What You Feel About Your Fiancé

How you view your fiancé affects how you listen to him/her. A partner's communication is colored by how you view him/her. This view may have been shaped by your observations of his/her past performance or by your own defensiveness.

Listen with Your Ears, Your Eyes and Your Body

If your fiancé asks, "Are you listening to me?" and you say, "Yes" while walking away or fixing dinner or doing the dishes, perhaps you aren't really listening. Concentrate on the person and the message, giving your undivided attention. Turn off the appliance or TV when there is an important matter to talk about; set aside what you are doing and listen.

There are several responses you could make to indicate to your spouse that you are listening and catching all of what he is saying.

First, clarifying is one of these responses. This response reflects on the true meaning and the intention of what has been said. "I think what you're saying is that you trust me to keep my promise to you, but you are still a bit concerned about my being away just before your birthday."

Second, observing is another skill. This response focuses upon the nonverbal or tonal quality of what your partner has said. "I noticed that your voice was dropping when you talked about your job."

Third, another response is reflective listening. A reflective statement attempts to pick up the feelings expressed. Usually a feeling word is included in the response, such as, "You seem quite sad (joyful, happy, delighted, angry, etc.) about that."

Fourth, inquiring is yet another helpful response. An inquiry draws out more information about the meaning of what was said. A very simple response would be, "I would like you to tell me more if you can."

Be Patient, Especially If Your Fiancé Is a Slow or Hesitant Talker

You may have a tendency to jump in whenever you can find an opening, finish a statement or hurry him/her along. You cannot assume that you really know what is going to be said. You cannot read another person's mind.

Listen to your fiancé in love. When you listen in love you are able to wait for the person to share his/her thoughts, feelings and what he/she really means.

10
COMMUNICATION GUIDELINES

Communication can be very complex or it can be quite simple and flow along easily for a married couple. Achieving quality communication, however, will take some thought and effort on the part of both of you. Over the past 10 years, as I have conducted marriage seminars and counseled numerous couples, several important issues have emerged. In this chapter we will consider several of the most important issues regarding communication and then conclude with a set of guidelines. If followed, these qualities will make your communication healthy and productive.

The Nature of Self Talk

We all carry on conversations with ourselves daily. This doesn't mean that we are odd or on the verge of spacing out. It's normal to talk to oneself. After you complete this chapter, however, I hope you will be much more conscious of your self talk. You will probably be shocked by the amount of time you spend on inner conversations and how those conversations affect your engagement and will affect your marriage.

Are you aware that:

- Most of your emotions—such as anger, depression, guilt, worry—are initiated and escalated by your self talk?
- The way you behave toward your fiancé is determined by

your self talk and not by his or her behavior?
- What you say and how you say it is a direct expression of your self talk?

Self talk is the message you tell yourself—the words you tell yourself about yourself, your fiancé, your experiences, the past, the future, God, etc. It is a set of evaluating thoughts about facts and events that happen to you. As events are repeated, many of your thoughts, and thus your emotional responses, become almost automatic. Sometimes the words you tell yourself are never put together in clear statements. They may be more like impressions.

Self talk or inner conversation is not an emotion or feeling. Neither is it an attitude. However, repeated sets of self talk *become* attitudes, values and beliefs. Attitudes are with us for a long period of time and may be inactive. Self talk represents the evaluating thoughts that we give ourselves at the present time. Your expressions of anger, ways of showing love and how you handle conflict are motivated by conscious and subconscious self talk. Your self talk may be based upon some of your attitudes. A positive attitude toward life would tend to generate positive self talk and a negative attitude, negative self talk. Self talk is different from our beliefs, yet it is often *based* on our beliefs.

Most people believe that outside events, other people and circumstances determine their emotions, behaviors and verbal responses. Actually, however, your thoughts are the source. What you think about these things and about people will determine the emotions you feel and the behaviors and verbal responses you express.

As an example of *your beliefs* affecting your self talk, consider these typical beliefs about marriage:
1. A spouse should make me happy.
2. A spouse should meet all of my needs.
3. A spouse should know what my needs are without my having to tell him/her.
4. A spouse should be willing to do things according to my way of doing them.
5. A spouse should not respond in an irritable or angry way to me.

Do you nurture any of these beliefs about your future marriage relationship?

Another example of the results of self talk can be seen in two different groups of people: those with a failure identity and those with a success identity. Each identity appears to be tied into the person's self talk. Positive self talk statements include the following: "I have value and worth as a person"; "I have accomplished much of what I have tried in the past"; "Trying a new venture is worthwhile"; "If something is new, I see it as a challenge and an opportunity for me to grow."

A failure identity can come from statements like "I'm not as capable as others"; "I will probably fail"; "I can't accomplish what I try"; "If I try I might fail and others will see my weaknesses."

Let's consider for a moment this exchange between a husband and wife and discover the self talk that prompted it.

Saturday morning, 11:00 A.M.

Wife   It's about time you got up. It looks like you're going to waste the entire day!

Husband   (looking a bit startled) What's with you? I'm just taking my time getting up and enjoying a day off.

Wife   That's just it. You're around here so rarely and half the day is shot! By the time you get dressed and cleaned up lunch will be over and nothing has been accomplished.

Husband   Who said I was getting dressed and cleaned up? The only thing I want to accomplish is a cup of coffee, the paper and the football game on TV!

Wife   What? Then the whole day is shot to . . . I don't get a day off. There's a whole list of work to be done here. When *are* you going to do it?

Husband   What? I suppose you've been saving up a list of work projects again. Why don't you give me some notice ahead of time? If I wanted to work today, I could go into the shop and get overtime plus some peace and quiet!

What is happening in this conversation? First of all, each person has an unspoken expectation for Saturday: one for work and one for pleasure. Many problems such as this could be eliminated if individuals clarified their expectations in advance. Let's look at the wife's self talk at this point. She was expecting her husband to accomplish a number of tasks on Saturday. She got up at 6:30. Note her inner conversation and the progression.

7:30 "I hope he gets up pretty soon. I'd like to get started on these projects. With the kids away today we can get a lot done."

8:15 "Boy! I don't hear a sound. Well, I'm going to start work in the yard. He'll probably hear me and then he can join me."

9:15 "What time is it? 9:15! I don't believe it! He's sleeping away the morning. Who does he think he is? How thoughtless! I ought to go in there and wake him up!"

10:00 "Just because he has no work at the plant or at church he thinks he's entitled to sack out. What about me? When do I ever get to do this? He ticks me off! He probably knows I want him to take care of those chores he's been putting off. He just wants to ignore them and me! Boy, is he going to hear from me. I'll let him sleep but he's going to pay a price for it!"

10:45 "And I was going to cook his favorite meal and dessert tonight. Fat chance of that. How could he be so insensitive? Look at all I do for him!"

What type of emotions do these statements arouse? What kind of behaviors do you think these statements prompt? What kind of communication is happening?

Suppose, instead, the wife chose self talk such as the following:

"I wish he would get up. I think I'll check and see if he's just resting or sleeping."

"I'm not sure he's going to get up in time to do much today. I'd better revise my list and then ask him if he could help me with these two chores after lunch."

"I am a bit upset with him but I have to admit I didn't tell him I wanted him to work today. Next time I'll talk it over with him and share my ideas before the weekend."

"I could serve him breakfast in bed when he wakes up. That'll knock his socks off! When's the last time I did that?"

Two different styles of self talk. The choice is yours whether to make your self talk positive or negative.

Many of your thoughts are automatic. You don't sit around thinking about what you are going to think next. Thoughts slide into your consciousness so smoothly that you don't even sense their entrance. Many of them are stimulated from past experience, attitudes and beliefs. You build up storehouses of memories and experience, retaining and remembering those things which you concentrate upon the most.

Whether they are automatic or consciously thought out, what are your thoughts like? Are they negative or positive? Most people who worry, are depressed, irritable or critical toward others have automatic thoughts that are negative.

A characteristic of negative thoughts is that they are generally wrong. They do not reflect reality. Often they reflect insecurity, feeling of inadequacy and fears. These alien invaders are not usually welcome guests. They are generally exaggerated negative conclusions about your future, your spouse, your marriage, your everyday life and yourself.

How to Control Your Thoughts

There are several basic ways to control your automatic thoughts and give yourself an opportunity to produce more positive communication. The first is to *become aware of these thoughts by keeping track of them*. Writing them on a piece of paper or a 3 × 5-inch card is one way to accomplish this. Another way to eliminate automatic thoughts is to *learn to counter or answer them*. Countering is bringing your thoughts to trial and examining the evidence. But you can do this only if you are aware of them. You need to catch the thoughts that come to your mind, and then, when you are aware of them, respond with a conscious thought. You need not settle for either your automatic thoughts or those you consciously work up. You can choose precisely what you will think about.

Here are some typical thoughts that will probably enter your mind at one time or another:

"My fiancé will never change. He/she will always be that kind of a person."

"I can never meet my fiancé's needs."

"If I bring up that subject, my fiancé will just get mad again."

"If I share what really happened, I'll never be trusted again."

"Why bother asking him/her to share his/her feelings? He/she will only clam up again."

"He hates me."

When a thought comes into your mind, what do you do with it? A negative or angry thought, when not challenged, intensifies and expands. In 1 Peter 1:13 we are told to "gird your minds for action." To "gird" requires mental exertion. Peter says that we are to eliminate or cast out of our minds any thoughts that would hinder our growth in our Christian life. This in turn will affect our married life. If you would like to learn more about self talk, please read *Do You Hear What You're Thinking* by Dr. Jerry Schmidt, Victor Books.

Emotions and Feelings

As I have conducted marriage enrichment seminars with thousands of couples across the country, many wives have shared the same concern: "Men do not share their emotions sufficiently." These women say they do not know *what* their husbands are feeling or *if* they are feeling. The husbands avoid being known. This appears to be true of a man's relationships with other men as well as women. See David Smith's excellent book *The Friendless American Male*, Regal Books.

Many men do not have a sufficient vocabulary to express their emotions. As they are learning to be men they learn to value expressions of masculinity and to devalue what they label "feminine" expressions. These men are locked up emotionally. They are not comfortable sharing their failures, anxieties or disappointments. An indicator of being a man is, "I can do it by myself. I don't need any help." Unfortunately this leads to the inability to say "help me" when help is desperately needed. Masculinity means not depending on anybody. Dependence is evaluated with being a parasite. These men resist being dependent. This often shows up in the man's obsession with his work, his inability to relax and play—unless he is in a highly competitive situation—and his struggle with weekends and vacations.

Many men think that all feelings are "weaknesses." Sympathy and empathy are awkward for them. Fear is one of the most difficult emotions for them to admit.

Some men (and some women) use their intellect as a defense against their feelings. They may dissect, analyze and discuss their emotions, but they do not spontaneously share them. Men and women have the same emotions. Men's emotions are not different from women's emotions. We simply differ in our expression of them. Many men are seen as totally cognitive or logical. Many women are seen as totally relational and feeling oriented. Could it be that we are actually both? Could it be that there are various forms of logic? Not everyone goes directly from A to B to C. Some leave A and make several side trips before coming back to B and then take several other side trips before arriving at C. Some go through this process in a few short words, others add descriptive adjectives and paint a beautiful mental picture.

One belief which some men hold is that being masculine automatically means being logical, analytical or scientific. The word *logical* means "capable of reasoning or of using reason in an orderly cogent fashion." Therefore intuition or the ability to sense or feel what is happening is not available to many men, for that seems feminine. They believe that logic and intuition cannot work together.

Warren Farrell raises an interesting question: "Must a person who expresses emotions think without logic or does it ultimately free one to think logically?"[1] Isn't it possible that a person who is in touch with his emotions and expresses them freely may see things accurately and make decisions logically and perceptively as well? Feelings are not to be feared but experienced and expressed. They are to be accepted as one of God's gifts and used to add greater depth to life. Feelings are to be used as an inner release.

Herb Goldberg, in his enlightening book *The Hazards of Being Male,* describes the destructive consequences for a man who does not express his emotions.

1. He is vulnerable to sudden, unpredictable behavior.
2. He denies his feelings and needs and then becomes resentful because intimates take him at face value and don't read his hidden self correctly.
3. He becomes prone to emotional upsets and disturbances.
4. He becomes prone to countless psychophysiological disorders.
5. The defenses against feeling force him further and further away from relationships.
6. His inability to ask for help means that when his defenses begin to shatter, he begins to withdraw further or turns to drugs or alcohol.[2]

Lack of emotional acceptance and expression is one of the contributions to a male mid-life crisis. A man was not created to deny his emotions. No one was. Neither were we created just to express our emotions and not use the cognitive ability God has given us. Some people's communication reflects a life devoid of correct thinking and feeling.

In His creative act God has given all of us different temperaments, talents, spiritual gifts, skills and motivations. Our culture and upbringing, however, can create a filter that keeps us from experiencing our full creation. Soon we begin to be molded to this world. But Paul tells us, "Do not be conformed to this world, but be transformed by the renewing of your mind, that you may prove what the will of God is, that which is good and acceptable and perfect" (Rom. 12:2, *NASB*).

Even if women are more prone to express their emotions and empathy, does the Word of God say that this is the way it was meant to be? Culture might tell us that emotions are female traits, but God's Word does not agree. Jesus expressed anger. He wept. He felt distress and was deeply depressed! In the Word of God we are called to experience various attitudes and demonstrate outward expressions of Christian growth and character. In the Sermon on the Mount Jesus says that those who are sorrowful, who possess a gentle spirit, who show mercy,

whose hearts are pure and who are peaceful are blessed. We are called to manifest the fruit of the Spirit which is love, joy, peace, patience, kindness, goodness, faithfulness, gentleness and self-control.

If we have learned certain patterns of behavior in the past, the good news is that we can also unlearn them and begin to respond in a new way. The result will be a change for the better in our ability to communicate.

Build Your Vocabulary

If you do not know how to share your feelings and emotions, obtain a synonym finder or thesaurus and begin to expand your vocabulary. When it comes time to share, give three or four descriptive sentences instead of a one-line summary. Your description should include at least one feeling or emotional word.

I mention the one-line summary because in the groups of married couples I mentioned earlier, a major complaint of the women is: "Men never give sufficient details. All they give is the summary." As one woman expressed it, "Jim is on the phone for 20 minutes talking to a friend. When he gets off and I ask him what they said, he gives me a one-line summation. I don't want the condensed version. I want the whole novel-length story! One day he came home and told me he had just run into one of our closest friends and the man's wife had had their baby early that morning. I asked him, 'Well, was it a boy or girl? How large was it? What time was it born? etc.' He said all he remembered is that they had their baby. He didn't remember all those trivial details!"

Another woman in a seminar suggested that "men tend to view communication like a telegram. Women view it as a meal to be savored." Men tend not to share many details in certain areas or about certain topics. But listen to us as we talk about what is important to *us!* Our work, our hobbies, our recreation, etc. Men can be just as detailed and precise as anyone else when they want to be. And they can express themselves in detail with emotion as well. I have heard communication of men that has moved me to tears. Each year I read dozens of novels and many of the authors are men. They paint word pictures in my mind that are a combination of facts, feelings and descriptive adjectives. We *are* capable.

A man who is more of a cognitive responder not only can build his vocabulary, he can begin to think out loud in the presence of his wife. He can say to her, "I'm going to just brainstorm out loud and what I say may not make complete sense or have continuity but I'm willing to try and describe my day differently for you." And as he does this his wife has the opportunity to listen and take in. She should not criticize, correct or make any value judgments about what he is saying.

A simple way to learn how to expand what we say is the *XYZ* method. X is the actual event you want to describe; Y are your feelings about the event; Z are the consequences or results of the event.

Instead of telling your fiancé, "I bought a new car today." Period. Try expanding on the topic: "Guess what I did. Boy, am I excited! I finally did something I've always wanted to do but was afraid to. I saw this new car on the lot that was just what we talked about three months ago. I saw the price, offered them $400 less and bought it. I feel great. In fact I feel like a kid again and it's a car I can afford! How would you like to take a ride with me tonight?"

Remember to share more than the event. People who care about you want to know your inner feelings as well as your thinking. If you make a decision about something, don't just share the decision. Share with your fiancé the process that led you to make that decision.

What can a woman do to help a man share his feelings?

A woman can do a number of things to help a man become more expressive, but the changes, if they do occur, will take time. You are battling years of conditioning, so beware of making demands that he can't meet as yet.

Barbara, an accountant, said, "When I wanted John to share, I wanted his feelings, but my requests came across as demands. And one day he told me so. I learned to be sensitive to his days and moods and whenever he began to share some of his frustrations I listened and listened well. He didn't want a dialogue or someone to solve his problem. He wanted to vent and I wanted to hear!"

Listed below are some suggestions on how women can help men learn to share their feelings. Some of the suggestions may sound familiar, others quite new. Remember, if what you're doing now isn't working, why keep using the same approach? A new approach used in a loving, consistent manner may help build the intimacy you're looking for.

Help your husband-to-be acknowledge that he has feelings inside of him and, that by learning to share these, the relationship will bloom. One man said, "After several months of being engaged I wondered why our relationship was so stale. And then I realized it wasn't the relationship, it was me! When Jan asked me questions or wanted to talk, I gave her thoughts and facts, but no feelings. She could have gotten the same from a computer. We decided to take 15 minutes a day to share. She agreed to summarize her three-minute descriptions into three or four lines. I agreed to share whatever I said with feeling words. It took us awhile to learn this new style, but what a difference it has made! I share—she listens—and we feel closer."

Try direct questions that encourage a direct response.

"I'd like to know the most interesting experience you had at work today (or this week)."

"When have you felt angry (sad, excited, happy or whatever) this week and what caused it?"

"I feel there's a portion of you I don't know. If I had to describe how you feel about your work, what would I say?"

"You really seem to enjoy your woodworking. What do you enjoy so much about it?"

"When you were a little boy, what were your greatest delights and your greatest fears?"

By asking thought-provoking questions about topics fairly comfortable to him—like work, hobby, childhood—you make it easier for him to communicate. These questions vary in their degree of comfort. Sometimes it's easier to pose a factual question first, then lead into how he feels about it. Most men find it easy to describe facts about work. But it may take them time to discuss the joys, frustrations or boredom of their jobs.

One woman asked her fiancé: "Honey, you know I enjoy hearing more details and feelings from you. Often it appears that you seem hesitant to talk to me about them. Is there something I do to make it difficult for you to share these with me?"

Another woman was more direct: "John, you know I like to hear the details, your feelings, the inner workings of who you are. I need this and the times you have shared with me were fantastic. You're so articulate and have such depth. You probably feel I pressure you or even nag you into opening up to me. I know you don't like it when I do slip into that trap. I want you to know that I'm not trying to nag. But I do appreciate your sharing more with me."

Develop an atmosphere of trust so he will eventually be able to express the entire gamut of feeling arising in him. If you ask your husband-to-be how he feels about his job and he says he hates it and wants to quit, your own feelings of insecurity may cause you to respond, "You can't! Think of our future!" And he won't be as open with you again. You don't have to agree with his feelings; the goal is not to debate, but to build communication and thus intimacy.

Thank him for sharing. Let him know how much it means to you and ask if there's anything you can do to make it easier for him. Ask what it is that you can pray about for him each day. This gives you something specific to talk about at the end of the day.

Often watching a movie together can open the emotional side of a person. A film can bring out feelings some people would ordinarily suppress. Emotions brought to the surface through the film seem "safe" because in a sense they are not "real." Discussing the movie later, using factual and feeling questions, may lead to a unique discussion.

What, then, is the answer to some of the complaints and concerns that men and women bring up about one another? The answer is *adjust, change* and *reinforce* any changes which occur.

Critical Communication Times

There are two extremely critical times for communication

between a husband and wife. Both times involve only four minutes! That's all. They are the first four minutes upon awakening in the morning and the first four minutes when you're reunited at the end of the day. These eight minutes can set the tone for the day and the evening. This is a time when couples can share their love, concern, interests and affirmation of one another; or they can be angry, curt, critical or indifferent and adversely affect the rest of the day or evening.

The second important time of the day also has a significant impact on a couple's relationship. What will happen during the first four minutes when you and your future spouse are reunited at the end of the day? Will it be a time of factual reports about the news, the weather or other bad news? Will it be a time of silence?

Some spouses complain that the family dog gets more attention than they do! And it may be true. Dogs are talked to, caressed, patted; they get their ears rubbed and their backs and chins scratched. Not a bad way to greet your spouse! Touching, asking feeling questions and expressing happiness in seeing the other person should make the evening better.

A positive greeting between husband and wife can have a positive impact on other family members as well. Here are several steps to take to enhance your evenings after you are married:

1. When you see each other at the end of the day, give each other your undivided attention and listen with your eyes as well as your ears.

2. Don't come in with a task-oriented checklist of "Did you do . . . ?" Your spouse may end up feeling like a hired hand.

3. Touch, kiss, hug, hold—whatever is pleasing to both of you.

4. Don't make your first statement to your spouse a complaint. It will put a damper on his/her anticipation of seeing you.

5. Create a relaxing time. Don't immediately hit your spouse with a list of chores to do. Don't breeze in and head directly for the phone, workbench or hobby.

6. Prepare yourself mentally to greet your spouse. Spend time thinking of what you will say and do. Rehearse it in your mind. At least one night a week plan a surprise greeting—something you rarely do or have never done before.
7. Attempt to look appealing to your spouse. A quick combing of the hair or swish of mouthwash will be appreciated.
8. You could phone one another before you leave work for the day. During this time you could discuss who has the greatest need to be met when you arrive home. Some days a wife may need a half-hour relief from the kids to restore her sanity. Both of you may need a half-hour to clear your minds (after the initial four minutes) before you're human again. You might even discuss how you would like to be greeted as you reunite at the end of the day.

Communication Rules and Guidelines

All of us have rules we abide by in communication and in resolving conflict. But seldom do we define or verbalize them. Some rules are positive and healthy. Others are negative, detrimental and continue to perpetuate communication problems.

If engaged couples would take the time to develop specific guidelines for communication and agree to follow them, communication could become a very positive experience. These guidelines help especially when there are differences of opinion.

A few years ago as I was working with a couple in premarital counseling, I discovered that they were having a bit of a struggle in the area of conflict. I suggested they develop a communication covenant to follow in their conversations. The next week they returned with several guidelines. I sent them out with the assignment to detail the steps involved in implementing each guideline. They returned with their list and then we spent some time refining and revising it.

Here is their covenant. Would these guidelines work for you in your future marriage?

Communication Covenant

This covenant will be read together each Sunday and then we will ask each other in what way we can improve our application of this covenant in our daily lives.

1. We will express irritations and annoyances we have with one another in a loving, specific and positive way rather than holding them in or being negative in general.
   a. I will acknowledge that I have a problem rather than stating that you are doing such and such.
   b. I will not procrastinate by waiting for the right time to express irritations or annoyances.
   c. I will pinpoint to myself the reason for my annoyances. I will ask myself why it is that I feel irritation or annoyance over this problem.
2. We will not exaggerate or attack the other person during the course of a disagreement.
   a. I will stick with the specific issue.
   b. I will take several seconds to formulate words so that I can be accurate.
   c. I will consider the consequences of what I say before I say it.
   d. I will not use the words *always, all the time, everyone, nothing,* etc.
3. We will attempt to control the emotional level and intensity of arguments. (No yelling, uncontrollable anger, hurtful remarks.)
   a. We will take time-outs for calming down if either of us feel that our own anger is starting to elevate too much. The minimum amount of time for a time-out will be one minute and the maximum 10 minutes. The person who needs a greater amount of time in order to calm down will be the one to set the time limit. During the time-out each person, individually and in writing will first of all define the problem that is being discussed. Second, the areas of agreement in the problem will be listed. Third, the areas of disagreement will be listed, and fourth, three alternate solutions to this problem will be listed. When we come back

together the person who has been the most upset will express to the other individual, "I'm interested in what you've written during our time-out. Will you share yours with me?"

b. Before I say anything I will decide if I would want this same statement said to me with the same words and tone of voice.

4. We will "never let the sun go down on our anger" or never run away from each other during an argument.

   a. I will remind myself that controlling my emotional level will get things resolved quicker and make me less inclined to back off from the problem.

   b. I am willing to make a personal sacrifice.

   c. I will not take advantage of my partner by drawing out the discussion. If we have discussed an issue for 15 minutes then at that time we will take a time-out and put into practice the written procedure discussed under Step 3.

5. We will both try hard not to interrupt the other person when he/she is talking. (As a result of this commitment, there will be no need to keep reminding the other person of his/her responsibility, especially during an argument.)

   a. I will consider information that will be lost by interrupting my partner.

   b. It is important that the person talking should be concise and to the point.

   c. I will remember that when I interrupt my partner, he/she won't be able to listen as well as if I had waited for my turn.

   d. I will put into practice Proverbs 18:13 and James 1:19.

6. We will carefully listen when the other person is talking (rather than spending that time thinking up a defense).

   a. If I find myself formulating my response while the other person is talking I will say, "Please stop and repeat what you said because I wasn't listening and I want to hear what you were sharing."

   b. If I am having difficulty hearing my partner, then, when he/she says something, I will repeat back what I

heard him/her saying and what I thought he/she was feeling.

7. We will not toss in past failures of the other person in the course of an argument.

   a. I will remind myself that a past failure has been discussed and forgiven. True forgiveness means it will not be brought up to my partner again.

   b. I will remind myself that bringing up a past failure cripples my partner from growing and developing.

   c. If I catch myself bringing up a past failure I will ask my partner's forgiveness and I will then state what I want the other person to do in the future and I will commit myself to this behavior.

8. When something is important enough for one person to discuss, it is also important for the other person.

   a. If I have difficulty wanting to discuss what my partner wants to discuss I will say to him/her, "I know this topic is important to you and I do want to hear this even though it's a bit difficult for me."

   b. In implementing this agreement and all the principles of communication in this covenant, we will eliminate outside interferences to our communication such as listening to the radio or television, reading books on our lap, etc. We will look at one another and hold hands during our discussion times.

DATE:

SIGNED:

SIGNED:

As I have shared these guidelines with others, some people have said, "Well, they worked that out when they were engaged. Just wait until the realities of marriage sink in."

Thirteen months after their marriage I saw this couple for their last session, as I do with all couples. Halfway through I asked them if they remembered the covenant they had developed previously. They said, "Oh yes, we take it out quite often for review. In fact we went through it two weeks ago and rated ourselves and each other on a scale of 1-5 for each item to see how we were doing. Then at the bottom of the covenant we wrote, 'This is what I'll do this next week to enhance the application of this covenant.'"

I had no further questions.

Twenty-Three Communication Guidelines

Here are a number of communication guidelines. Read through them and then commit yourself to follow these when you are married:

1. Greet your spouse after a period of being separated (even if only for a few hours) with a smile, pleasant talk such as a happy greeting, touching and kissing, a compliment, humor or recounting one of the day's interesting or "success" experiences.

2. Set aside a period of transition between work—or any potentially stressful activity—and other parts of the day. This transition time is designed to provide a "decompression period" so that any pressures, frustration, fatigue, anger or anxiety that may have been generated will be less likely to affect marital communication. Some people pray as they drive home, committing the day's activities to the Lord. Others visualize how they are going to respond to each family member. Some couples take 20 minutes when they arrive home to sit in a dimly lighted room and listen to a favorite record with very little talking.

3. Never discuss serious subjects or important matters that involve potential disagreement when you or your spouse are overly tired, emotionally upset, sick, injured or in pain.

4. Set aside a special agreed-upon time every day to take up issues involving decision making, family business, disagreements and problems. This "Decision Time" should allow for the relaxed and uninterrupted discussion of all decision-making and problem-solving activities. No other activities should be involved, such as eating, driving or

watching television. Take the phone off the hook. It may also help to set a time limit.

5. Some couples have found it helpful to save all complaints about their marriage, disagreements and joint decisions for the scheduled Decision Time when these matters are taken up. Jot down items as they arise. When you pose a problem or lodge a complaint, be specific as to what you want from the other person. Do you want anger, defensiveness, resistance and continuation of the problem? Or openness, cooperation and a change on the part of the other person? The way you approach the problem will determine your spouse's response.

Example: "You are not involved enough with the children."

Better to say: "I appreciate the time you spend with the children and so do they. I know you have a lot going on but we would all appreciate your evaluating your schedule so you could spend more time with them."

Example: "You are never affectionate."

Better to say: "I enjoy the times when you touch me. I would appreciate it if you would touch me and hold me several times a day and also let me know if you like something I'm doing."

Recognition and praise of what another person has done is necessary to his/her sense of self-worth. It also opens the door for a person to accept a constructive suggestion.

6. In the decision sessions, try to reach a specific solution.
7. Set aside a scheduled time for noncontroversial marital conversation, every day if possible. Among the topics that could be discussed are: the experiences you each have had during the day or at other times; noncontroversial plans or decisions that involve individual partners, the two of you as a couple or the whole family.
8. Each person should have a special "topic turning signal" to signal his or her spouse to change the conversation from a controversial topic. The signal should be an agreed-upon neutral word or phrase.
9. Do not blame your partner. Save matters of complaint and proposed change for the Decision Time.

10. Stay on the topic being discussed until each of you has had a say.
11. Avoid talk about what happened in the past or what might happen in the future if it is potentially controversial.
12. Be specific in what you talk about. Define your terms and avoid overstatement and generalities.
13. Acknowledge the main points of what your partner says with words such as "I see," "I understand," "Yes," "Um-hm."
14. Try to keep the nonverbal aspects of your communication consistent with the verbal message. Don't express compliments with scowls or an indifferent tone of voice. Have a pleasing facial expression.
15. Be as accurate as you can in describing objects or events for your partner. Remember, you are describing it from your perspective.
16. Praise your spouse for the things he/she says that you like. Use words that you think will be appreciated.
17. Discuss topics with your partner that you know he/she will like to talk about. If your partner fails to discuss topics to your liking, do not hesitate to suggest that you would like to discuss the desired subjects further.
18. Never exaggerate in order to make a point. If you really want to persuade your spouse, write the subject down and save it for the next Decision Time.
19. Don't mind-read or make presumptive statements about what your partner has said.
20. Don't quibble about minor or trivial details.
21. Respond fully but not excessively when your turn comes.
22. Repeat what you think your partner said if you have trouble understanding him/her or if you think you did not hear what he/she intended.
23. Help each other to follow the rules. Praise your spouse for rule-consistent talking.

11
COMMITMENT TO RESOLVE CONFLICTS

"What causes conflicts and quarrels among you? Do they not spring from the aggressiveness of your bodily desires? You want something which you cannot have, and so you are bent on murder; you are envious, and cannot attain your ambition, and so you quarrel and fight. You do not get what you want, because you do not pray for it. Or, if you do, your requests are not granted because you pray from wrong motives" (Jas. 4:1-3, *NEB*).

These strong words were written to Christians many years ago, yet they are words that are applicable today. Many marriages are characterized by strife and bickering rather than peace and harmony. Couples who have developed harmony are not those who are identical in thinking, behavior and attitudes—they are not carbon copies of each other. They are the couples who have learned to take their differences through the process of acceptance, understanding and eventually, complementation. Differing from another person is very natural and normal and adds an edge of excitement to a relationship. How do you settle differences now? How will you settle differences when you are married?

Because each person is unique and because what each brings to the marriage is unique, conflict will emerge. In fact, there will be numerous conflicts throughout the life of the marriage. This is not bad; this is normal. How you respond to the conflicts and

deal with them is the real issue.

Let's define conflict. "Conflict, . . . to strike together. 1. a fight, clash, contention. 2. sharp disagreement of opposition as of interests, ideas, etc., mutual interference of incompatible forces or wills.[1]

One of the traditional ways couples learn to deal with conflict is to suppress it—try to forget it, sweep it under the rug or shrug it off. This so-called nice way has been equated with being Christian. Burying conflicts, however, only builds resentments that drain you of energy and color your entire perception of daily life. When differences are buried, they are buried alive and at some time will resurrect themselves.

Another way couples handle conflict is to express their feelings unreservedly. For some couples this approach resembles a war. Wave after wave of attack seems to mount and the intensity increases. In time, verbal garbage is thrown, computer memories are activated (and these would put an elephant's memory to shame) and total frustration is the end result. During this time each assumes the role of a skilled lawyer, eager not only to indict the other but to see him/her convicted (and in some cases hung!).

So let us look more closely at marital conflict. Marriage is the coming together of two unique and different individuals in order to share life with each other. Their differences are quite unavoidable. They have lived separate lives for perhaps 20 to 25 years, during which each has developed a set of individual tastes, preferences, habits, likes and dislikes, values and standards. It is totally unreasonable to suppose that two people, just because they are married to each other, should always want to do the same thing in the same way at the same time.

> This doesn't happen even with identical twins. So the couple have differences of opinion and of choice, and these differences lead to disagreements. The couple may be quite willing to do the same thing in the same way, but at different times; or to do the same thing at the same time, but in different ways. How do you solve this problem? Either they must give up the idea alto-

gether, and both feel frustrated and blame each other; or one will have to give up his particular wish and do it in the way, or at the time, the other wishes. People in love are able to do a good deal of giving up and giving in because love creates a generous mood. But sooner or later a situation develops in which neither is willing to accommodate the other because patience is exhausted, or enough ground has already been surrendered, or this time it is a matter of principle. So they are deadlocked, and now we have a conflict.[2]

Unresolved conflicts do not diminish but continue to grow and grow. Notice the progression as indicated in the following chart.[3]

Difference of opinion	"Spat"	Confrontation
Heated debate or argument	"Quarrel"	Division
Intense physical anger	"Fight"	Rejection
Hostility confirmed	"War"	Separation

Differences and disagreements in marriage is the rule and not the exception. Every couple at one time or another will be angry and have arguments and complaints against each other.

Conflict has been called *a positive sign of marital growth*. Do you agree? Perhaps not, if conflict in your experience has been overly painful, unresolved or buried. But some areas of conflict are to be expected at various stages in the life cycle of a marriage. Marriages pass through stages of development as people do. Think of the potential differences or conflicts that can emerge when:

• The first child is born.
• The second child is born.
• A spouse has to work 12 hours a day while the other is home with three preschoolers.
• A child has an accident while under the supervision of one of

the parents and the insurance does not cover the $600 medical bill.

- The last child leaves home.
- Retirement comes and both are now at home.

Think of some of these differences between the two of you. Are they potential for conflict?

- One is a bottom-of-the-toothpaste-tube squeezer and the other squeezes from the top.
- One wants the toilet paper rolled from the top of the roll and the other wants it rolled from the bottom.
- One's body temperature cries for the thermostat to be set at 78 degrees and the other is constantly flinging open the windows.
- When they speak, one gives an entire novel-length story and the other gives a two-line news summary.
- One is a night person and the other a morning person.
- One wants the room absolutely dark for sleeping and the other wants a light on.
- One feels that making love belongs only in the bedroom in the dark and under the covers, but the other likes variety and is quite inventive.
- One tosses and hangs the clothes wherever he feels led and the other has the clothes color-coded and on the hangers a half-inch apart.
- One likes to arrive 15 minutes late and the other 15 minutes early.

    1. List eight minor or subtle differences between the ways you and your fiancé think, believe and do things.

    2. Now go back over your list and check those that may create conflict in your marriage.

    3. Which of these differences are really important and significant?

4. What major conflicts have you experienced in your relationship so far?

What Is Conflict?

In the chart earlier in this chapter the word "quarrel" was indicated. Many couples state that what pains them most about conflict is the constant quarreling that occurs. Other couples say they avoid conflict, if at all possible, because of the biblical teaching concerning quarreling. What does the Bible say about conflict? What does it say about quarrels? Are quarreling and conflict synonymous? Not really. Many conflicts are handled and resolved without quarreling.

A quarrel has been defined as verbal strife in which angry emotions are in control and the couple does not deal with the issue but instead attacks the other person. This behavior creates strain in their relationship. The Scriptures tell us not to be involved in quarrels: "It is an honor for a man to cease from strife and keep aloof from it, but every fool will be quarreling" (Prov. 20:3, *AMP*). "As coals are to hot embers, and wood to fire, so is a quarrelsome man to inflame strife" (Prov. 26:21, *AMP*). "Let all bitterness and indignation and wrath (passion, rage, bad temper) and resentment (anger, animosity) and quarreling (brawling, clamor, contention) and slander . . . be banished from you" (Eph. 4:31, *AMP*).

Let us consider some basic assumptions about conflict.

Conflict is a natural phenomenon and is therefore inevitable. Conflict arises in part because all of us perceive people and situations differently. These different perceptions allow for different opinions and choices which can cause conflict. And conflict is inevitable between people who care about each other and want to develop a deeper relationship. Dwight Small says:

The most frequent conflicts husbands and wives experience are verbal. Verbal conflict in itself is not harmful; any damage it causes depends upon the maturity of the two people in conflict. Entirely different ends can be served by a verbal clash, and some of them are healthy and good. Conflict can open doors of communication as well as shut them. As a reality in marriage, conflict can be creatively managed for good; it is part of the growth process. Don't ever underestimate its positive possibilities![4]

In Christian marriage, conflict—with its demand for confession, forgiveness and reconciliation—is a means God employs to teach humility.[5]

Conflict indicates a deprivation in some personal value or need. Every human being has some very basic needs. William Glasser suggests that the most basic are the need to love and be loved, and the need to feel worthwhile. Abraham Maslow describes a hierarchy of needs: we strive to fulfill our physiological needs first, then our safety needs, our need for love and belongingness, need for esteem and self-actualization needs. When you have a conflict, consider which of your needs are not being met.

Conflicts usually emerge as a symptom. When people find themselves in conflict they usually have some need that is unfulfilled. Resolving the conflict may not solve the problem. It is better to look below the symptom, discover what need the person is striving to fulfill and resolve the need rather than the symptom only.

Most conflict is not dealt with openly because most people have not been taught effective ways of resolving conflict. Many couples ignore minor conflicts to keep from rocking the boat. When a major conflict arises, people tend to avoid it because they have not learned how to deal with minor conflicts. They have not developed the necessary skills by solving minor problems.

Urban G. Wiese and Bernard R. Steinmetz say about conflict:

Disagreements are inevitable at many points in mar-

riage and family living. Sometimes spouses become competitors as well as helpers and complements to one another. Rather than the isolation and alienation which accompanies conflict too often in the home, couples need to overcome the loneliness, to reduce the personal hurt, retaliation and recrimination. To accomplish this, differences must be brought out into the open so that good communication can be restored. Angry reactions are inevitable in a person's life, but the most important consideration is what one does with anger.[6]

Conflict provides opportunity for growth in a relationship. Conflict is like dynamite. It can be helpful if used in the right way but can also be destructive if used at the wrong time or in the wrong manner. Through conflict a person can share his differences with another individual. Facing conflict is also a way of testing one's own strength and resources. Each person in a conflict situation will bring one or more alternative choices to the discussion. These can be explored together, and each can learn from the other. When the conflict is resolved, there can be growth on the part of both individuals.

Again, Dr. Small states: "Disagreements come and they must be handled in one way or another . . . We must also make the distinction that the disagreements are one thing, behaving disagreeably is quite another."[7]

Unresolved conflicts interfere with growth and satisfying relationships. Barriers are erected when conflicts are not resolved. We tend to become defensive in order not to be hurt. A defensive reaction places a strain on any relationship.[8]

Jesus experienced conflict. He was in constant conflict with the religious leaders of Judea. They wanted to defeat Jesus. They wanted to win over Him. John 8:1-11 is an account of one of the conflicts between Jesus and the religious leaders. You are probably familiar with the story. Here is a paraphrase of the story:

Early next morning Jesus returned to the Temple and

all the people there gathered around him as he began to teach. Then the scribes and Pharisees brought in a woman caught in adultery. They stood her before Jesus and said, "Teacher, this woman was caught in the very act and in the Law, Moses said we are to stone such a woman to death. What do you say?" They did this as a trap to catch Jesus in some break with the Law, so they could charge him . . . But Jesus responded, "Let him among you who has never sinned throw the first stone at her . . . " And when they heard what he said they went out one by one, leaving the woman standing there before Jesus. Then Jesus stood up and spoke to her. "Where are they all? Has no one condemned you?" And she replied, "No one, sir." "Neither do I condemn you," said Jesus. "Go home, and do not sin again."[9]

Jesus did not run or withdraw from this confrontation. Neither did He yield to their demands nor did He compromise, but forced the scribes and Pharisees to consider an alternative—mercy for the woman.

All of us, upon entering marriage, develop a style of dealing with conflict. We might assume that our spouse will handle conflict in a similar manner, but there are many ways of handling conflict. These differences are at the heart of much of the conflict.

David and Vera Mace suggest that the conflict process looks like Diagram 1.

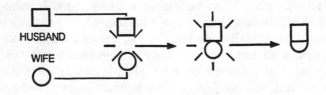

DIFFERENCES ► DISAGREEMENT ► CONFLICT ► RESOLUTION

Diagram 1

First we see the difference between husband and wife, illustrated by different shapes—a square and a circle. Next we see the difference in their wishes brought close together as a result of their desire for mutual involvement, which leads to a disagreement—each asking the other to yield.

If they continue to confront each other in a state of disagreement, frustration is stirred in both and a state of emotional heat develops. This is a conflict. They are moving into a clash of wills, a quarrel, a fight.

What they do next is critical. If they can't tolerate conflict, they will disengage and go back to where they started. The difference remains unresolved. The disagreement is recognized but avoided in the future, and the feelings of frustration suppressed. The attempt to become more deeply involved with each other, in that particular area of the relationship, is abandoned.[10]

It is interesting to note that it is not "the longer couples are married the more they have to talk about." It is more accurate to say that "the longer couples are married the more they learn what *not* to talk about." And in doing this they erect barricades, which soon are reconstructed into walls and they live with certain areas of isolation between them. But there is another way of approaching conflict, which the Maces described:

But suppose now that they recognize conflict as a friend in disguise and let their emotions heat up. And suppose that, instead of getting in a fight, they examine these hot emotions and try to understand their own and each other's feelings. It will then be possible to turn the conflict to good account by working together to resolve the original difference by some kind of adjustment or compromise. This is shown in the diagram as a figure that is a combination of the square and the circle.[11]

Dealing with Conflict

There are five basic ways of dealing with marital conflict.

The first way is to withdraw. If you have a tendency to see conflict as a hopeless inevitability and one which you can do little to control, then you may not even bother trying. You may withdraw physically by removing yourself from the room or environment, or you may withdraw psychologically by not speaking, ignoring or insulating yourself so much that what is said or suggested has no penetrating power. There are many who use the backing-off approach to protect themselves.

Winning is another alternative. If your self-concept is threatened or if you feel strongly that you must look after your own interests, then this method may be your choice. If you have a position of authority and it becomes threatened, winning is a counterattack. No matter what the cost, winning is the goal.

People employ many different tactics in order to win. Since married couples are well aware of each other's areas of vulnerability and hurt, they often use these areas to coerce the other person into giving in to their own demands. "Winners" may attack self-esteem or pride in order to win. They may store up grudges and use them at the appropriate time in order to take care of a conflict. They may cash in old emotions and hurts at an opportune moment. The stockpiling approach is another form of revenge and certainly does not reflect a Christian's demonstration of forgiveness.

If winning is your style, answer the following questions:

1. Is winning necessary to build or maintain your self-esteem or to maintain a strong picture of yourself?

People need strong self-esteem in order to find satisfaction in life and in their marriage. But what is the foundation upon which this is built? If one is insecure or doubtful, he often creates a false image to fool others and in the process confuses himself. To defer to another, to give in or to lose a debate or argument is a strong threat to the person's feelings about himself, and thus he fights so that this will not happen. The authoritarian person is not usually as secure as the image he portrays. Deferring to another is a sign of a weakening of his position.

2. Is winning necessary because you confuse wants with needs?

The spouse who feels he needs something may be more demanding about getting it than if he just wants something. Do you distinguish between needs and wants? You may see something as a *need* in your life but your partner may see it as a *want*. How do you know if something truly is a need?

A third approach to handling conflict is yielding. We often see yield signs on the highway; they are placed there for our own protection. If we yield in a conflict, we also protect ourselves. We do not want to risk a confrontation so we give in to get along with our partner.

We all use this approach from time to time, but is yielding a regular pattern for you? Consistent yielding may create feelings of martyrdom or eventually guilt in your partner. We even find some individuals who need to "lose" in a marital conflict. This approach is a face-saving way of doing that. By yielding, you give the appearance that you are in control and are the one behaving in the "most Christian" way.

We learn to suppress or repress our anger and pile it up instead of doing what Nehemiah did when he heard of the mistreatment of the poor people. "I [Nehemiah] was very angry when I heard their cry and these words. I thought it over, then rebuked the nobles and officials" (Neh. 5:6-7, *AMP*). Some people gain as much from defeat as others do from winning.

Another method of dealing with conflict is compromising or giving a little to get a little. You have discovered that it is important to back off on some of your ideas or demands in order to help the other person give a little. You don't want to win all the time, nor do you want the other person to win all the time. This approach involves concessions on both sides and has been called the "horse trading" technique.

A fifth method is called "resolve." In this style of dealing with conflicts, a situation, attitude or behavior is changed by open and direct communication. The couple is willing to spend sufficient time working on the difference so that even though some of their original wants and ideas have changed, they are very satisfied with the solution they have arrived at. Diagram 2 shows a way of diagramming the five styles of handling conflict.

Five Conflict Styles

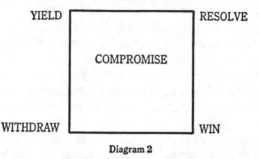

Diagram 2

Which method of handling conflict is best or ideal? Each one has an element of effectiveness in certain situations. At times, compromise is not the best whereas winning may be. Yielding on certain occasions can be a true and pure act of love and concern. But the ideal style that we work toward is that of resolving conflicts.

Let's look at Diagram 3.

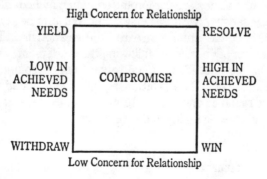

Diagram 3

You will notice that some new descriptive words have been added to Diagram 2. When a person uses *withdrawal* as his normal pattern of handling conflict, the relationship suffers and it is difficult to see needs being fulfilled. This is the least helpful style of handling conflicts. The relationship is hindered from growing and developing.

If this is your style, think about why you withdraw. It is not a demonstration of biblical submission or meekness. This method is often employed out of fear—fear of the other person or of one's own abilities.

Winning achieves the individual's goal but at the same time sacrifices the relationship. A person might win the battle but lose the war. In a marriage, personal relationships are more important than the goal and winning can be a hollow victory.

Yielding has a higher value because it appears to build the relationship, but personal goals or needs are sacrificed in yielding, which can breed resentment. Yielding may not build the relationship as much as some believe, because if the relationship were that important, a person would be willing to share, confront and become assertive. What can be accomplished through resolution will build the relationship even more and show a greater concern for the relationship than do other methods.

Compromising is an attempt to work out the relationship and the achievement of some needs. The bargaining involved may mean that some values are compromised. You may find that you are not very satisfied with the end result, but it is better than nothing. This could actually threaten the relationship. There may be a feeling of uneasiness following the settlement.

Resolving conflict is the ideal toward which couples are encouraged to work. The relationship is strengthened when conflicts are resolved and needs are met on both sides. It takes longer and involves listening and acceptance.

A Christian response to disagreements includes a willingness to be patient in working out a solution.

The willingness to exchange information, feelings, and ideas with one another leads to mutual understanding. Our first idea about a problem will not always be the same as our later understandings of it. As new ideas are expressed and the discussion develops, the issues may change.[12]

You may have changed in the process, but you are glad for the change. It is positive and beneficial. And change is possible and necessary! Because Jesus Christ is present in your life, you can give up your fears and insecurities. You can have a new boldness and courage to confront the issues of life and, in a loving manner, others around you. Some people feel that it is impossible for them to change. But the Word of God says, "I can do all things through Christ which strengtheneth me" (Phil. 4:13, *KJV*).

Resolving Conflict

You may have decided that you would like to have *resolve* as your style but are wondering what to do to bring that about. Here is a suggested format to help move you to the style of resolve rather than to the other four. These suggestions will work if you spend time, make the effort and persevere. Since conflict relates to the process of communication, and since it is impossible to separate the two, many of these suggestions are basic principles of communication. They are not necessarily listed in order of importance.

Speak directly and personally to the other person. Don't assume that the other person knows what you are thinking or feeling. If anything, assume that he/she knows very little and that this is his/her first time to deal with the issue. "In the end, people appreciate frankness more than flattery" (Prov. 28:23, *TLB*).

Be honest in your statements and questions. Ephesians 4:15 and 23 are important to practice both in making statements and in asking questions. When you ask a question, does your fiancé have the freedom to share his/her honest response? Even if you disagree with his/her response? If you feel that your partner has a double message behind his/her question or has an ulterior motive, respond only to the question at its face value. Don't get caught up in mind-reading or second-guessing.

Make statements out of your questions. Too often in a conflict one or the other feels as if he/she is in an inquisition.

Focus on your desired expectations or positive changes rather than on faults, defects or what you hope to avoid. This helps each of you become aware of what is gratifying and helpful to the other. Believe it or not, psychologically it is easier to begin new behavior than to terminate old behaviors. Don't apologize for your feelings or your needs.

When you are sharing what you want in a conflict, *share your request in a statement of preference* rather than a statement of necessity.

When you feel unloved by your partner, *initiate loving behavior toward the person.* If you begin to perform loving acts, your fiancé may act more loving toward you, but if not, that's all right; your act of love can fulfill some of your own needs and be a demonstration of Christ's love.

Make "I" statements rather than "you" statements and share your *present* feelings rather than your past thoughts or feelings.

Select an appropriate time. "A man has joy in making an apt answer, and a word spoken at the right moment, how good it is" (Prov. 15:23, *AMP*).

Define the problem. How do you define the problem and how does your partner? You could suggest that you both stop talking and write down exactly what it is that you are trying to resolve.

Define the areas of agreement and disagreement in the conflict. Share with the other person first of all what you agree with him/her about, and then ask what he/she disagrees with you about. Writing the areas of agreement and disagreement on paper help clarify the situation.

Here comes the difficult part. A few conflicts may be just one-sided, but most involve contributions from both sides. *Identify your own contribution to the problem.* When you accept some responsibility for a problem, the other sees a willingness to cooperate and will probably be much more open to the discussion.

The next step is to *state positively what behaviors on your part would probably help and be willing to ask for his or her opinion.* As your partner shares with you, be open to his or her feelings, observations and suggestions. Watch out for defensiveness!

Consider the following passages from *The Living Bible:*

"If you refuse criticism you will end in poverty and disgrace; if you accept criticism you are on the road to fame" (Prov. 13:18).

"Don't refuse to accept criticism; get all the help you can" (Prov. 23:12).

"It is a badge of honor to accept valid criticism" (Prov. 25:12).

"A man who refuses to admit his mistakes can never be successful. But if he confesses and forsakes them, he gets another chance" (Prov. 28:13).

Learning to resolve conflicts early in your relationship will lessen the pain and frustration and create the harmony you are seeking.

12
COMMIT YOURSELF TO CONTROL ANGER

As you look forward to your marriage, you have no intention of allowing anger to erode and wreck your relationship. I've never met any couple who planned to do this. Yet, many marriages today are destroyed by anger out of control. Anger is a part of life—including married life. Like it or not, you will become angry. In fact, I'm sure you've already been angry with your fiancé. Anger is an emotion given to man by God Himself. Our problem is that we don't handle anger very well. We tend to become angry for the wrong reason or we tend to express angry feelings in a hurtful or damaging way, rather than trying to help others and ourselves.

Who makes you angry? You do! Situations and other people cannot make you angry. No matter what your future spouse does, he or she does not make you angry. You create your own anger.

Anger, like other emotions, is created by your own thoughts. If your fiancé fails to follow through with a commitment he/she has made to you, you may become angry. Your anger comes from your thoughts about the meaning or significance you have given to his/her failure to follow through.

What Creates Anger?

There are many ways we create our own anger. *We may*

label our partner in some way because of what he/she has or has not done by thinking (or even verbalizing): "You jerk"; "You selfish person"; "You inconsiderate clown." But in doing so we tear him/her down. His/her good points are discounted. All you see is this one event and any others similar to it and you pass over the things you love about your fiancé.

Sometimes we become angry when our self-esteem is threatened. Perhaps your fiancé insulted or criticized you. You may not feel loved or liked and that feeling makes you angry.

Anger can also be generated by mind reading. In your mind you create your own reasons for why your fiancé or spouse did what he or she did and you project those reasons onto him.

"That's his mean nature. He's just like his father."

"She just wants to argue for the heck of it."

"Anyone who acts like that must not have any love or compassion."

But mind reading never works. You cannot know for certain the thoughts and motivations of another person. Mind reading only creates additional conflicts.

Inappropriate should/shouldn't statements create highly flammable fuel for your anger. Whenever you say, "You shouldn't (or should) have done that" you create the setting for anger. What you are doing is interpreting a situation a certain way and saying it should have been different. When you insist on holding onto the "shoulds," you keep yourself festered and upset. It would have been nice if the other person had performed as you wanted, but he or she didn't. Your anger won't change the past and probably will do little to alter the future. Consider the following two situations:

Situation 1: The house is a mess; especially the kitchen. John's wife is gone and he decides he is going to treat his wife by cleaning the living room, family room and kitchen. He vacuums, sweeps, dusts and washes dishes for two hours. "Wait until she sees this. Will she be surprised! She'll go wild with appreciation." So he hopes.

Sometime later his wife, Janice, arrives home with bags of groceries and clothes. She staggers into the house and drops the bags in the living room.

"John, would you bring in some of the groceries for me, please? There are so many and I'm beat. Wait until you see the great prices I found on clothes at Penney's. And guess who I saw . . . "

And so it goes for the next hour. Janice never mentions one word about the clean rooms. And after her whirlwind entrance the house soon looks like a hurricane had swept through. By now John is doing a slow burn. His anger has reached the boiling point. Is it her behavior that creates John's anger? Or is it his own thoughts? Let's enter his mind to see what he is thinking.

"She should have noticed all this work I did for her."

"She should have thanked me."

"She shouldn't have been so insensitive and inconsiderate."

"What a lousy way to treat me."

"She shouldn't have messed up these rooms."

"Just wait until she wants me to help her! Fat chance."

John's thoughts are making him feel hurt and angry. He *could* have thought:

"I wish she would notice the work I've done."

"Perhaps I did all this for what I would get out of it instead of just helping her."

"I can get along without her noticing. If not, I'll just ask if she noticed anything. I could let her know I have a better understanding of what housework is like."

"Next time I'll find a creative way to let her know her work has been done for her."

This series of thoughts is much more realistic and less emotionally charged. Changing "should" statements to "I wish . . . " or "it would be nice if . . . " will help us use our minds to control our emotions so we can maintain the ability to reason.

Situation 2: Curt was frustrated when he came in for counseling. He was livid with anger at his wife. "You bet I'm angry," he said, "and I've got a right to be. If you had to live with that hypocritical woman you'd be angry too. Oh, she puts on a great performance. She responds with love, kindness, patience and fairness with everyone else. But at home it's just the opposite! Everyone at church sees her as a saint! Ha! At home she's constantly griping, complaining, running me down and comparing me to others. If there's a fault to be found with me, she'll find it. She makes life miserable for me and I'm burned up. And don't tell me I don't have a right to be angry. I'm ready to take a walk on her!"

Curt had many expectations for Susan which (from his point of view) were not being fulfilled. As we talked we discovered that Curt not only had expectations but felt he had a right to demand that she fulfill those expectations. Curt was telling himself that:

1. It is wrong and terrible to be treated by my wife in this way, especially when she demonstrates Christian love to others.
2. I am correct in demanding that she treat me different from what she does.
3. She owes me love and a submissive attitude since she is my wife.
4. She is terrible to treat me this way.
5. She should change her response to me.

Curt's self talk and expectations were creating his anger. As we continued to explore his feelings we discovered that he felt as if he was wasting his life with Susan and he wasn't sure that she could change. He believed that (most of the time) he was loving, kind and considerate with Susan and thus she should respond in like manner.

Curt had three causes for his anger: (1) expectations; (2) a list of shoulds and oughts for Susan; (3) a pattern of self talk that fed his anger.

Dealing with Anger

---

1. If you were counseling Curt what suggestions would you give him for dealing with the above three causes?

2. What new statements would you ask him to make in his mind that would help him with his anger?

The *American Heritage Dictionary* describes anger as a strong, usually temporary displeasure, but does not specify the

manner of expressions. You can be just as angry while keeping silent as you can while yelling at someone.

The words "rage" and "fury" are used to describe intense, uncontained, explosive emotion. Fury is thought of as being destructive, but rage can be considered justified by certain circumstances.

Another word for anger is "wrath"—fervid anger that seeks vengeance or punishment. "Resentment" is usually used to signify suppressed anger brought about by a sense of grievance. "Indignation" is a feeling that results when you see the mistreatment of someone or something that is very important to you.

A simple definition of anger is "a strong feeling of irritation or displeasure."

What can you do with your anger? There are several steps you can take to lessen anger and reduce inner tension.

Identify the cause. Your anger is a symptom, the tip of the iceberg. Underlying thoughts or other feelings are creating your sense of irritation.

What are your thoughts? Are you applying labels to your fiancé? Are you trying to mind read? Are you operating on the basis of "shoulds" or "should nots"? Are you feeling hurt over some situation? Is there something that you are afraid of? Identify your fear.

What are you frustrated over? Frustration is one of the biggest causes of anger. If you're frustrated you probably have some unmet needs and expectations—probably unspoken.

Evaluate the reason for your anger. Is your anger directed toward your partner because he did something intentionally and knowingly to hurt or offend you? How do you know it was intentional?

Write out your responses to these questions: How is your anger helpful or useful? Is it going to help you build your relationship or reach the goal that you want?

Apply Nehemiah 5:6-7. In order to reduce your anger you need some practical application of Nehemiah 5:6-7 *(NASB):* "Then I was very angry when I had heard their outcry and these words. And I consulted with myself [or thought it over], and contended with the nobles and the rulers and said to them, 'You are exacting usury, each from his brother!' Therefore, I held a great assembly against them."

One way to "consult with yourself" is to make a list of the advantages and disadvantages of feeling and acting in an angry manner. Consider the short-term and long-term consequences of the anger. Look over the list and decide what is the best direction to move.

Another approach is to identify the hot thoughts and replace them with cool thoughts. Hot thoughts are the anger-producing thoughts. David Burns describes a situation in which a couple had disagreements over the husband's daughter from a previous marriage. Sue, the wife, felt that Sandy, the daughter, was a manipulator and led John around by the nose. No matter what Sue suggested he ignored her. As Sue pressured him, John withdrew from her. Sue became more and more upset and angry. Then Sue made a list of her hot thoughts and substituted cool or calm thoughts.

Hot Thoughts	*Cool Thoughts*
1. How dare he not listen to me!	1. Easily. He's not obliged to do everything my way. Besides he is listening, but he's being defensive because I'm acting so pushy.
2. Sandy lies. She says she's working, but she's not. Then she expects John's help.	2. It's her nature to lie and to be lazy and to use people when it comes to work or school. She hates work. That's her problem.
3. John doesn't have much free time and if he spends it helping her, I will have to be alone and take care of my kids and myself.	3. So what. I like being alone. I'm capable of taking care of my kids by myself. I'm not helpless. I can do it. Maybe he'll want to be with me more if I learn not to get angry all the time.

4. Sandy's taking time away from me.	4. That's true. But I'm a big girl. I can tolerate some time alone. I wouldn't be so upset if he were working with my kids.
5. John's a schmuck. Sandy uses people.	5. He's a big boy. If he wants to help her he can. Stay out of it. It's not my business.
6. I can't stand it!	6. I can. It's only temporary. I've withstood worse.[1]

1. List some of the hot thoughts you experience.

2. Write out a replacement or cool thought.

3. What do you become angry at the most?

What You Need to Know About Anger

The Scriptures teach a balanced perspective on anger. We are to be angry at times, but for the right reasons. We are always to be in control of the intensity and direction of our anger. It is not supposed to dominate us or run out of control. Revenge, bitterness and resentment are not to be a part of our life. We are to recognize the causes and our responsibility for our anger. We are never to deny our anger or repress it, but eliminate it in a healthy manner.

What happens outside of us—external events—do not make us angry. Our thoughts do, whether they are automatic thoughts or ones we choose to think. Realizing that you are responsible for your anger is to your advantage. You have an opportunity to take control of your thoughts and your emotions. In most situations your anger will work against you and not for you. It can cripple you and make you quite ineffective. Anger can limit your capacity to discover creative solutions. If no real solution is available, at least you can free yourself from being dominated by the situation and give up resentment. Can joy, peace and contentment reside side-by-side with your anger?

If you're angry at your fiancé it could be that you believe that he/she is acting in an unfair or unjust manner. By looking at your expectations and beliefs you can lessen your anger. What we label unfair or unjust may be *our* evaluation alone.

Much of your anger may be your way of protecting yourself from what you see as an attack against your self-esteem. If someone criticizes you, disagrees with you or doesn't perform according to your expectations, your self-esteem may be threatened. Why? Because of what others have done? No. Because of your negative thoughts.

You and I have three choices for our anger: (1) we can turn it inward and swallow it, absorbing it like a sponge; (2) we can ventilate it; or (3) we can stop creating it. Let's look first at what happens when we swallow it.

Turning anger inward against yourself can give you hypertension, high blood pressure, ulcerated colitis or depression. When you repress your anger your stomach keeps score. Joseph Cooke describes what happens when we internalize our anger:

> Squelching our feelings never pays. In fact it's rather like plugging up a steam vent in a boiler. When the steam is stopped in one place, it will come out somewhere else. Either that or the whole business will blow up in your face. And bottled-up feelings are just the same. If you bite down on your anger, for example, it often comes out in another form that is much more difficult to deal with. It changes into sullenness, self-pity, depression, or snide, cutting remarks.[2]

Bottled-up or repressed anger may emerge in some nondirective ways. When it does, the angry person does not have to admit anger or take responsibility for it. This nondirective expression is usually referred to as passive-aggressive. The person's behavior can manifest itself in several ways. Forgetting is very common: "Are you *sure* you asked me?" or "Are you *sure* that was the time we agreed upon?" If you are the one who asked the question, you begin to wonder and doubt yourself. Actually, you have been set up!

Sarcasm is a "nice" way to be angry. A person is given two messages at one time—a complaint and a put-down. "You look so young I didn't recognize you." "Your new suit is sure radical but I like it."

Being late is another frustrating experience for the one against whom the anger is directed. This behavior may emerge unconsciously—the person is on time to some events but late to others.

Passive-aggressive behavior is unhealthy because: (1) it can become an ingrained pattern of behavior which can last a lifetime; (2) it can distort a person's personality; (3) it can interfere with other relationships.

Another choice is to ventilate all your anger. This may help *you* feel better but the results may not be very positive. And the person on whom you vent your anger certainly won't feel better!

A third choice is to stop creating your anger and/or to control the expression of your anger. How? By changing your thought life.

"Conscious delay" is a procedure you can use to hold back angry responses or any negative response that has been generated in the mind. It is possible to edit negative thoughts (which is not the same as denying or repressing them) so that you will express yourself or behave in a positive manner. It is not hypocritical nor is it dishonest to edit your thoughts. Ephesians 4:15 states that we are to speak the truth in love. A literal translation of this verse means that we are to speak the truth in such a way that our relationship is cemented together better than before. Totally blunt, let-it-all-hang-out honesty does not build relationships. By editing, you are aware of your thoughts and feelings and you are also controlling them. You are actually taking the energy produced by the anger and converting it into something useful that will build the relationship.

How is it possible to edit my thoughts when I begin to become angry? First of all, make a list of some of the things your fiancé does that cause you to respond with anger.

1. My fiancé is usually late, as much as 15 or 20 minutes. Whenever this happens I become angry.
2. My fiancé frequently overspends what he/she earns.
3. My fiancé leaves books, personal items and dishes around the house consistently and expects others to pick them up.
4. Often when I set up an outing or a date for us (even well in advance) my fiancé has already planned something for that time and does not tell me in advance.

Write the following questions on a piece of paper and carry it with you. As you find yourself starting to get angry, take a brief timeout and look at your list.

1. What are some things that make me angry? How do I usually think when these things occur?

2. What self talk do I use?

3. What are some of the possible explanations for the way my fiancé is behaving?

4. Am I guilty of the same problem or a similar problem? Have I attempted to be constructive and positive in any of my discussions with my fiancé about this problem? Will what I am about to say or do reduce the chance of my fiancé repeating the same behavior?

5. What are three alternate statements I could make to my fiancé to replace my usual response?

The Word of God has much to say about anger and uses a number of words to describe the various types of anger. In the Old Testament, the word for anger actually meant "nostril" or "nose." In ancient Hebrew belief, the nose was thought to be the seat of anger. The phrase "slow to anger" literally means "long of nose." Synonyms used in the Old Testament for anger include ill-humor and rage (Esth. 1:12), and overflowing rage and fury (Amos 1:11). Anger is implied in the Old Testament through words such as revenge, cursing, jealousy, snorting, trembling, shouting, raving, and grinding the teeth.

Several words are used for anger in the New Testament. It is important to note the distinction between these words. Many people have concluded that the Scripture contradicts itself because in one verse we are taught not to be angry and in another we are admonished to "be angry and sin not." Which is correct and which should we follow?

One of the words used most often for anger in the New Testament is *thumos,* which describes anger as a turbulent commotion or a boiling agitation of feelings. This type of anger blazes up into a sudden explosion. It is an outburst from inner indignation and is similar to a match which quickly ignites into a blaze but them burns out rapidly. This type of anger is mentioned 20 times (see Eph. 4:31 and Gal. 5:20). We are to control this type of anger.

Another type of anger mentioned only three times in the New Testament, and never in a positive sense, is *parorgismos.* This is anger that has been provoked. It is characterized by irritation, exasperation or embitterment. "Do not ever let your wrath—your exasperation, your fury or indignation—last until the sun goes down" (Eph. 4:26, *AMP*).

Acceptable Anger

The most common New Testament word for anger is *orgē*. It is used 45 times and means a more settled and long-lasting attitude of anger that is slower in its onset but more enduring. This kind of anger is similar to coals on a barbecue slowly warming up to red and then white hot and holding this temperature until the cooking is done. This kind of anger often includes revenge.

There are two exceptions where this word is used and revenge is not included in its meaning. In Ephesians 4:26 *(NASB)* we are taught to let not "the sun go down on your anger." Mark 3:5 records Jesus as having looked upon the Pharisees "with anger." In these two verses the word means an abiding habit of the mind which is aroused under certain conditions against evil and injustice. The type of anger that Christians are encouraged to have is the anger that includes no revenge or rage.

Rage interferes with our growth and our relationships. Rage produces attacks (verbal or physical), tantrums and revenge. It can destroy other people first and then ourselves.

Resentment is another loser. It breeds bitterness and can create passive-aggressive responses. Resentment can actually destroy us and, in time, other people as well.

There are four healthy reasons for controlling anger.

First, *the Word of God tells you to control it.* Note the reasons given in these verses:

"Do not be quick in spirit to be angry or vexed, for anger and vexation lodge in the bosom of fools" (Eccles. 7:9, *AMP*).

"He who is slow to anger is better than the mighty, and he who rules his own spirit than he who takes a city" (Prov. 16:32, *AMP*).

"He who has no rule over his own spirit is like a city that is broken down without walls" (Prov. 25:28, *AMP*).

"The beginning of strife is as when water first trickles [from a crack in a dam]; therefore stop contention before it becomes worse and quarreling breaks out" (Prov. 17:14, *AMP*).

"Good sense makes man restrain his anger, and it is his glory to overlook a transgression or an offense" (Prov. 19:11, *AMP*).

"Cease from anger and forsake wrath; fret not yourself; it tends only to evil-doing" (Ps. 37:8, *AMP*).

"Make no friendships with a man given to anger, and with a wrathful man do not associate, lest you learn his ways and get yourself into a snare" (Prov. 22:24-25, *AMP*).

These are just a few of the passages:

A second reason for controlling anger is *the effect that anger has on your body.* Your heart rate increases, bowels and stomach tense up, blood pressure increases, lungs work harder, your thinking ability lessens. A continual pattern of anger can make your body wear out more quickly. Stifled anger can create irreversible damage.

A third reason *concerns the sharing of the gospel.* How will others respond to your faith if you are known more for your anger than for your love?

The last reason for avoiding anger is that *it interferes with your own growth and the development* of relationships with others.

What If My Fiancé Is Angry with Me?

"My biggest problem," John said as he sat quietly near me, "is that I don't know what to do or how to act when Jean is angry with me. I either withdraw and crawl into a cocoon or I explode viciously. Neither response solves the problem!"

You and I will always live around people who become angry with us. Here are some suggestions for handling their anger.

1. Give the other person permission in your own mind to be angry with you. It is all right. It isn't the end of the world and you can handle it.
2. Do not change your behavior just to keep your fiancé from being angry with you. If you do you are allowing yourself to be controlled. If your fiancé becomes angry it is his/her responsibility to deal with it.
3. Do not reward your fiancé for becoming angry with you. If the person yells, rants, raves and jumps up and down and you respond by becoming upset or complying with what he/she wants you to do, you are reinforcing his/her behavior. If he/she is angry but reasonable, respond by continuing to state your point in a caring logical manner.
4. Ask the person to respond to you in a reasonable manner. Suggest that your fiancé restate his/her original concern, lower his/her voice and speak to you as though you had just been introduced for the first time.
5. If your fiancé is angry you do not have to become angry also. Read back over the Scriptures we listed and apply them to your life.

If anger interferes with your communication, there are several ways you can change the pattern.

Identify the cues that contribute to the anger. It is important to determine how and when you express anger. What is it that arouses the anger? What keeps the anger going? What is it that *you* do in creating the anger and keeping it going? Focus only on your part and don't lay any blame on your partner.

One way to accomplish this is by the use of a behavioral diary. Whenever anger occurs, each of you needs to record the following:

1. The circumstances surrounding the anger such as who was there, where it occurred, what triggered it, etc.
2. The specific ways you acted and the statements you made.
3. The other person's reactions to your behaviors and statements.
4. The manner in which the conflict was eventually resolved.

Establish ground rules for "fair fighting." See the chapters on communication for information on ground rules. Each of you will need to make a firm commitment to follow through in keeping these rules.

Develop a plan of action for interrupting the conflict pattern. This plan should involve immediate action to disengage from the conflict. It should also be a way to face and handle the problem at a later time. Interrupting the conflict is an application of Nehemiah 5:6-7 *(AMP)*: "I [Nehemiah] was very angry when I heard their cry and these words. I thought it over, then rebuked the nobles and officials."

Even the neutral expression of the phrases, "I'm getting angry," "I'm losing control," "We're starting to fight," "I'm going to write out my feelings," is a positive step. Upon hearing one of these statements, the other spouse could say, "Thanks for telling me. What can I do right now that would help?"

A commitment from both of you not to yell or raise your voices and not to act out your anger is essential. We call this "suspending" the anger. Agree to return to the issue at a time of less conflict. Most couples are not used to taking the time to admit, scrutinize and then handle their anger.

The interruption period could be an opportune time for you to focus upon the cause of your anger.

Ask your fiancé for help. This step is the clincher. Without it, not much progress can be made. The anger may die down, but that is not enough. Both of you need to find out just why one got mad at the other. If you do not, it could happen again, and again, and again. Your request for help is not likely to be turned down. It is in your fiancé's best interests to find out what is going on and correct it if a loving relationship is going to be maintained. When the request for help is accepted, the stimulus that caused the anger is usually completely neutralized and the negative emotion dissolves away. Then the work can begin right away, if possible, or at some agreed upon future time. The whole situation can thus be calmly examined and some solution found. In fact, conflicts between loving people are not really destructive. Rightly used, they provide valuable clues that show us the growing edges of our relationship—the points at which we need to work together to make it richer and deeper.[3]

De-cue your fiancé. If you have certain behaviors that tend to provoke anger from your fiancé, you should eliminate those behaviors so that he/she has no reason to retaliate. Minor or even defensive behaviors can be a trigger. Forgetting to call you, bringing up the past or criticizing your hairstyle are triggers that are easy to change. If a fiancé cowers and this elicits abusiveness, he/she can leave the room before the abuse occurs. In determining the cues it may be important to talk through some of these episodes to discover specific triggers and then to seek alternatives.

Change the faulty thinking patterns that affect the relationship. Here again the problem of expectations and assumptions arises. The faulty beliefs will need to be exposed and challenged. Some common themes are:

"You won't love me if I tell you how I really feel."

"You won't love me if I disagree with you."

"It's better just to hide how I feel."

"It's better just to fake it and go along with what he wants."

"Even if I do speak up, you'll win anyway."

"He should know what I need."

"All anger is wrong so I'm not going to express any."

"I'm not going to lower myself and get angry as he does."

Analyze and challenge the assumptions and eliminate any mind reading.

Redirect your focus from "who is right or wrong?" to "what are the behaviors involved and how do they affect our relationship?"

Each partner usually tries to remove his/her own guilt. You may look, therefore, for a scapegoat rather than evaluate your own part in the problem. If you can succeed in placing blame, then your own sense of responsibility is lessened. One person attacks, the other person counterattacks. Eventually both become proficient combatants. Each struggles under the pain of self-criticism.

Most people do not need to refine their blaming skills. Rather, they need to find new ways to avert placing the blame.

There are several practical steps you can take:

1. Instead of blaming or attacking your fiancé, share your own inner hurt and feelings. Hurt is usually where the blame is coming from.
2. When you have calmed down sufficiently enough to share complaints in a constructive manner, discuss some of the principles of communication or conflict resolution.
3. It is sometimes difficult, but very necessary, to distinguish between the person and his/her negative behaviors. This eliminates labeling the person as "bad" or "destructive."
4. If your fiancé suggests that you intentionally behaved in a negative manner, you could pose the question, "How would you respond if you knew that what happened was unintentional?" The person's accusation suggests that he/she is more of an expert on you than he/she really is. Give him/her an opportunity to put himself/herself in your shoes.

The Prayer of an Angry Person

Loving God, I praise You for Your wisdom, for Your love, and for Your power. Thank You for life, with its joys and mysteries. Thank You for emotions—including anger.

Forgive me when I am led by my anger instead of being led by You. Make me aware of the things I do that produce anger in others—help me change those things. Show me how to clean up the offenses I commit toward others, and give me the courage to ask forgiveness.

Help me to be able to look past the anger of another person and see Your creation in them, and to love them. Teach me how to forgive; and give me the humility to forgive gracefully.

Arouse me to oppose justice and other evils. Show me how to channel my energy that might otherwise be wasted in anger into constructive action in Your service.

You ask me to minister to persons around me. Help me understand what that means. Wake me up. Help me recognize that every moment of my life is an opportunity for Your love to flow through me.

Thank You heavenly Father, for Your love. Thank You for sending Christ so that we might have life and have it to the full, and for sending the Holy Spirit to comfort and guide us through the uncertainties and confusion of everyday living.

In Christ's name, Amen.[4]

13

COMMITMENT TO BUILD POSITIVE IN-LAW RELATIONSHIPS

Communication between engaged couples is one thing. But what about communication between you and your parents—yours and your fiancé's? And how will your future in-law/parent relationship affect communication between you and your fiancé now and after you are married?

By now you have grasped the importance of past relationships and experiences. The old relationship with your own parents and the new relationship with your prospective in-laws will have a definite effect on your marriage. Positive and healthy relationships with your in-laws and parents are possible. Let's consider some of the areas of potential conflict or harmony.

Those "Touchy" Traditions

Each partner brings to the marriage different customs, traditions and life-styles. In the home in which you were raised there were housekeeping practices, cooking styles and family customs that may differ from those of your fiancé. You may believe that the way your parents did things was the right way. Christmas holiday customs are a common example. Your fiancé may have been raised in a home where the tree was trimmed the week before Christmas, the presents were opened on Christmas Eve and a turkey dinner was eaten in early afternoon on Christmas Day. Your family may have trimmed the tree on Christmas Eve, opened the gifts the next morning and sat down to a ham dinner in the evening.

What about those this-is-the-way-we-always-did-it customs that are part of your background and which bring uncomfortable feelings and even conflict if you are asked to change them? Who should compromise? Which family tradition should you adopt? Should a newly married couple always fit into the established family customs of their parents? Or should they begin to develop their own? If you *always* go to her parents' home for Christmas, what would happen if you wanted to go to your parents' or to a friend's home? Do you always have pumpkin pie for Thanksgiving? What happens if you suggest a change? Who makes the gravy for the turkey dinner? And whose recipe is used for the dressing? These sound like small items but they can become major problems if they are part of a family's traditions. Can anyone rationally hold that the practices of one family are "right" and the other's are "wrong"? And how do you communicate to your parents or future in-laws that you want to change some customs or start new ones?

One of the major reasons married couples come for counseling is because of conflict with their in-laws. There is hurt, bitterness and misunderstanding. Often one partner feels caught in the middle between his parents and his spouse. Sometimes one or both spouses have not left home psychologically. After marriage, however, a couple's primary allegiance is to each other and not to his or her parents!

Sources of Conflict

There are several factors that can affect the relationship between couples and in-laws.

The ages of the couple in comparison with the ages of the parents are a possible source of conflict. A very young couple who had not made a break from home before marriage by living elsewhere or attending college in another location is faced with this adjustment. At the same time they are faced with the adjustment of learning to relate to another person in a marriage relationship.

Most parents of young couples are middle-aged and still involved in their own careers and achievements. They have interests and rewards apart from their married children. If they have assisted their children into adulthood, they may be looking forward to responding to their children as adults on an equal basis.

But some parents *demand* attention from their children, such as those with a declining income, few outside interests, chronic illness or very old age. If the parents divorce, their relationship with their grown children may also be affected.

1. Are you or your parents in any of these categories? If so, describe the effect it has had on you and will probably have on your marriage.

2. How has this situation affected communication with your fiancé?

3. What needs to be done to remedy the situation?

4. Describe how and where you would like to spend your first Thanksgiving and Christmas after you are married. Is this your decision or someone else's? Have you shared this with your fiancé? Your parents?

A person's birth order in the family can influence his relationship with his future in-laws. If one spouse is the oldest child in a family and the other the youngest, this difference may affect their marriage relationship and also the expectations of their parents and in-laws. The parents of the youngest child may be somewhat reluctant to let go of their last child. The parents of the oldest child may have higher expectations for their son-in-law or daughter-in-law.

1. Where are you in the birth order of your family?

2. How will this affect your marriage?

Couples and their parents often have unrealistic expectations of what a relationship should be between themselves. One set of parents may have imagined a close, continuing relationship between themselves and their new son-in-law or daughter-in-law. They assume they will all get together every weekend, call every third day and enjoy all Thanksgivings and Christmases together. They are also certain that the young couple will never live more than five miles away so they can have constant contact with their grandchildren. And they expect at least four grandchildren, the first within two years!

But what if you have other plans? What if you plan on not having any children, living 2,000 miles away and writing your parents once a month? These expectations need to be openly discussed as soon as possible.

What happens when one person comes from a family with close and warm relationships and the other does not? The latter may not want to establish a close relationship with his future in-laws. Or the opposite might be true. The person who had little or no warm, close times at home may seek a close relationship with the future in-laws. The one whose family was close may want to break away!

A newly married couple's choice of where they live can influence their relationship with the in-laws. Couples who live with their parents are only asking for increased conflicts. The young couple will feel restricted in many ways. The wife, particularly, will feel out of place in her mother-in-law's home. When a couple lives with one set of parents, the other in-laws may get jealous and want to do some "controlling" of their own.

What about the life-style and goals of the couple and their parents? Highly affluent, work-oriented parents often have a difficult time restraining themselves from exerting pressure on their married children who may have a different standard of living. The problem is intensified if the couple consistently criticizes their parents' standards.

What differences and similarities do you see in your life-style and goals and those of your parents and future in-laws?

And then there is the area of grandparents and grandchildren. Some parents look forward to becoming grandparents and have their own ways of pressuring a couple to "produce." Other parents resent being grandparents because it makes them feel old. If a child does not look like the grandparents, is not the sex they were hoping for or does not behave according to their expectations, conflicts may arise. A frequent complaint in this area is the way grandparents treat their grandchildren when they come for a visit. Some grandparents overindulge or spoil their grandchildren, making discipline that much harder for the parents when the children come back home. And what if the grandchildren prefer one set of grandparents over the other and want to spend time with them and not with the others?

Here are some typical adjustment difficulties that can occur. How would you communicate with your spouse or your in-laws in order to resolve these problems?

Case 1: A husband judges and criticizes his wife's housekeeping. He keeps referring to how his mother did it and uses her example as a standard. Or a wife continues to refer to her relationship with her own father as a model of what a dad does with his children.

Case 2: John's parents constantly criticize him and his wife. They have an opinion for everything, especially how to raise the children. These unsolicited comments are beginning to frazzle John and Betty's nerves. How can they constructively confront John's parents with the problem?

Case 3: Harry's parents are very demanding in a manipulative way. They want attention and have many expectations regarding Harry and Tina's time. When they don't get their way they try to make Harry and Tina feel guilty. Here is a portion of their conversation with Harry. How would you respond to some of these statements?

Mom: Hello, Harry, this is Mom.

Harry: Hi, Mom, how are you doing?

Mom: Oh, all right I guess. (She sighs.)

Harry: Well fine, but how come you're sighing?

Mom: Oh, well, I guess I haven't been doing so well. Anyway are you coming over this weekend? I was hoping to see you. You know it's been several weeks since you and Tina were here.

Harry: I'm sorry you're not feeling well, Mom. No, we won't be coming over this weekend. We have some other things that we have already planned to do.

Mom: Well, what's more important than seeing your dad and mom? Aren't we important to you anymore? Well, we sure are disappointed. We were positive that you would be over and I already have a turkey for dinner. Did you know that? You know your brother and sister come over to see us all the time. We don't even have to ask them! A good Christian son wants to see his parents often. If you really loved and cared for us, you would want to come and see us.

Case 4: The husband says: "Every year we have to spend our vacation with my wife's parents. We've done this for the past eight years! And it's not the most relaxing experience either. I feel stuck but what else can we do? They *expect* us to come! I'd like to see some other parts of this country."

Case 5: Another common problem is that of parents who feel they must contact their son or daughter every day. For example, a wife was really bothered because of constant mothering by her mother-in-law. Each day the mother would call and want to know how her son was doing at his job, whether he was gaining or losing weight, eating the right food, whether he had stopped smoking yet, etc. This was a situation in which the mother-in-law needed to stop making the phone calls in order for the wife to feel better. How would you handle the situation?

Here are some possible ways to handle the situations just described.

Case 1: If the wife's cooking (or housekeeping, driving, ironing, etc.) is being compared with her mother-in-law's, she might say something like, "Honey, one of the things I would really appreciate and that would make me feel better is for you to let me know when something I've cooked for you pleases you. I do feel hurt when I hear about your mother's cooking all the time. I want to develop my own cooking skills, but I need positive feedback from you."

Or the husband might say, "Honey, I would really appreciate it if you could let me know when I have done something that helps you as you work with the kids. I really become discouraged when I keep hearing about how your dad always did such and such when you were growing up." Both of these statements contain positive and specific comments that are the proper ways to share concern and complaints.

Case 2: This can be a delicate situation which most of us would prefer avoiding. We are afraid of the outcome although we dislike the constant criticism. We are concerned over the potential hurts and anger of our parents if we confront them. Remember that you are confronting them because you care and want a better relationship. If you do not confront them and request a change, in all likelihood your relationship will die. Here are some ways you might confront them.

"I would really appreciate your sharing some positive things about what's going on with you."

"When you have a complaint, I would really appreciate it if you would also suggest something positive that you feel we are doing."

"When we are disciplining the children, I would appreciate your not saying anything about what we are doing in front of them. I am always open to positive suggestions but please share them with me later, when they are not around."

Case 3: Here is the actual entire conversation that Harry had with his mother. This may be a totally different way of responding for you, but Harry's persistence and nondefensive responses were effective.

Mom: Hello, Harry, this is Mom.

Harry: Hi, Mom, how are you doing?

Mom: Oh, all right I guess. (She sighs.)

Harry: Well, fine, but how come you're sighing?

Mom: Oh, well, I guess I haven't been doing too good. I don't know what's wrong. Anyway, are you coming over this weekend? I was hoping to see you. You know it's been several weeks since you and Tina have been here.

Harry: I'm sorry you're not feeling too well, Mom. No, we won't be coming over this weekend. We have some other things that we have already planned to do.

Mom: Well, what's more important than seeing your mom and Dad? Aren't we important to you anymore?

Harry: I can understand that you want to see us, Mom, and you are important, but we won't be coming over this weekend.

Mom: Well, we're sure disappointed. We were positive that you'd be over and I already have a turkey for dinner. Did you know that?

Harry: No, Mom, I didn't.

Mom: Both your father and I are disappointed. Here we were expecting you two to come and we have the turkey already bought.

Harry: Mom, I can tell that you're disappointed but

we won't be able to be there this weekend.

Mom: You know your brother and sister come over to see us all the time. We don't even have to ask them!

Harry: That's true, Mom. They do come over more and I'm sure they're a lot of company. We can plan for another time and work it out in advance.

Mom: A good Christian son wants to see his parents often.

Harry: Does my not coming over make me a bad Christian son?

Mom: If you really loved and cared for us you would want to come and see us.

Harry: Does my not coming to see you this weekend mean that I don't love you?

Mom: It just means that if you did, you would be here.

Harry: Mom, not coming over doesn't mean I don't care for both of you. I love you and Dad. But I won't be there this time. I'm sure you can use the turkey now or freeze it. Now, let me check with Tina and we'll look at our schedule to see when we can all get together.

Case 4: Vacations with in-laws can be a problem. One spouse can become irritated and may come away very upset after a lengthy visit. A solution might be to engage in some enjoyable activity elsewhere while his mate visits her own parents alone. This may seem to contradict what people have been taught or what seems to be right. But if the extended stay does not promote better relationships between in-laws and does not have a positive effect upon the marriage, this may be the only solution. I am not suggesting that a spouse never visit his in-laws. But many couples have found the answer to be infrequent visits for brief periods of time.

Another possible solution is to shorten the entire visit. If one person would like to visit his/her parents for a month and the other feels uncomfortable with being there that long or being separated from his/her spouse for that long, they could compromise. Make the visit for only two weeks. It might also be best not to visit in-laws or parents every year on your vacation. This could create a tradition which you may find difficult to change later on. It also limits your possibilities of enjoying other vacation experiences.

Case 5: Constant contact initiated by the parents may reflect many needs on their part—loneliness, control, a need to be needed, etc. A couple needs to be in agreement as to the approach to take to resolve this particular conflict. They could agree on a goal and then communicate this goal to his mother: "Mom, we do enjoy hearing from you but there really is no need for you to call each day. Why don't we arrange our calls in this way: If we need something or something is wrong we'll be sure to call you. We also would like you to have opportunity to develop other relationships and not be so dependent on us. You know that you are always invited for dinner on Sunday. Why don't you plan to see us on Sundays and call us just on Wednesdays? That way we can stay in touch on a regular basis. In case of emergency you know you can always call."

Principles from Scripture

The ideal pattern for any relationship is found within Scripture. In any situation or relationship we need to visualize the Word of God in practice in our lives. As you read the passages below, begin by asking yourself, "How do I see myself actually doing what this passage says to do?" Then visualize several practical scenes. After each passage write out how you see yourself responding to your future in-laws or parents.

1. "Let all bitterness and wrath and anger and clamor and slander be put away from you, along with all malice. And be kind to one another, tender-hearted, forgiving each other, just as God in Christ also has forgiven you" (Eph. 4:31-32, *NASB*).

2. "Pursue after peace with all men, and the sanctifications without which no one will see the Lord. See to it that no one comes short of the grace of God; that no root of bitterness springing up causes trouble, and by it many be defiled" (Heb. 12:14-15 *NASB*).

3. "Blessed are the peacemakers, for they shall be called sons of God" (Matt. 5:9, *NASB*).

4. "If possible, so far as it depends on you, be at peace with all men" (Rom. 12:18, *NASB*).

5. "Walk . . . with all humility and gentleness, with patience, showing forbearance to one another in love" (Eph. 4:1-2, *NASB*).

One of the goals of our family relationships is harmony with unity. As people get in the habit of being open, honest and truthful with one another, deeper relationships develop. But hard work is involved.

Paul wrote, "Make my joy complete by being of the same mind, maintaining the same love, united in spirit, intent on one purpose" (Phil. 2:2, *NASB*). We might define these mandates as follows:

• "Being of the same mind"—intellectual unity

- "Maintaining the same love"—social unity
- "United in spirit"—emotional unity
- "Intent on one purpose"—volitional unity.

Improving Your In-Law Relationships

Here are some specific steps you can use to improve your in-law relationships. It is vital that both you and your future spouse discuss and apply these together.

Take a positive, optimistic view of your in-law relationships. There are many stereotypes about in-laws, but we need to move beyond these biased perspectives.

Mothers-in-law are not always a curse; often they are a blessing.

Couples do not always find it impossible to live with or near their in-laws; some do so and enjoy it.

Men are not more frequently annoyed by their in-laws than are women. There are actually more conflicts between the husband's wife and his mother!

Keeping quiet about in-law problems is not the best way to deal with them. It is far more preferable to clear up differences as they arise.

A person does not have to feel helpless about his in-law relationships; there is much that can be done to make them satisfactory. We must become willing to take risks, however.

Recognize the importance of your fiancé's family early in your relationship. Any attempts to ignore future in-laws just increases friction.

Evaluate which customs from your family background you want and what new ones you would like to try or to establish. Communicate these to your parents and in-laws. You may want to change customs every few years. Let parents and in-laws know that you will do this. Remember that as married adults *you* will have as much to say about what to do on Thanksgiving and Christmas as your parents and in-laws do.

Consider the needs of your parents and your fiancé's parents at this time in their lives. Often the reason people behave in the way they do is because they are trying to fulfill some particular need. But their behavior may not accurately reflect what their needs really are and thus we are confused. Have you ever considered that the suggestions which come from parents may reflect some of their own needs? They may not really be attempts on their part to control your lives or interfere.

A young woman shared this experience. Whenever her mother would come over to her home she would constantly check the house for dust and dirt. One day after this woman had worked for hours cleaning the house and scrubbing the floor, her mother came for a visit. As the mother sat in her daughter's kitchen, her eyes spotted a six-inch section of woodwork next to the tile which her daughter had missed. She mentioned this to her daughter. The daughter could feel the anger slowly creeping up through her body and her jaw tensed and her face became red.

Her mother noticed this reaction to her comment and said, "Honey, I can't really be of much help to you in anything else, but this is one thing I can help you with." As she shared, the daughter realized that her own mother felt inadequate and useless around her and this was her only way of attempting to feel useful and needed. Both mother and daughter now have a better understanding of each other.

Most parents need to feel useful, important and secure. They still like attention. What could you do to help them fulfill these needs? After you are married ask your in-laws outright what you could do to help them feel useful. It may take just a few simple actions and the expression of concern on your part to help your in-law feel important and loved.

Treat your future in-laws with the same consideration and respect that you give your friends. If they are Christians, can you see them not just as future in-laws but as fellow members of the Body of Christ? Can you see them as brothers or sisters in Christ? If they are not Christians, can you see them as individuals for whom Christ died? Can you remember that God's love is an unconditional commitment to imperfect people? See their potential in the same way God sees them.

When your future in-laws show an interest in some area of your life and give advice, respond just as you would if a friend were giving you some advice. If it is good advice, follow it and thank them for their concern. If it is not what you want to do, thank them for their suggestion but continue doing what you had planned to do in the first place.

Some couples say, "But you don't know my future in-laws or my parents! They won't give up! They keep on and on, and if one approach doesn't work they will try another or they will try to divide my fiancé and me on the issue!" Perhaps they will, but honest and firm assertiveness on your part will be helpful. They may continue to press because it has worked for them in the past. If you remain firm and consistent, they will learn that you have the right to respond to the advice and suggestions as just that—advice and suggestions, not absolute laws.

Give your future in-laws the benefit of the doubt. If they seem overly concerned with your affairs, it could be that they are really concerned with your welfare. They may not be trying to interfere in your life. Could your past experience or self talk be influencing your current response?

Look for positive qualities in your future in-laws. Too often we tend to focus on the faults and weaknesses of others and overlook their positive traits.

When you visit your future in-laws (and when they visit you), keep the visits reasonably short. Be sure you have plenty to do when you are there. Be as thoughtful, courteous and helpful as you can be. Consider them as you would your friends.

When you marry, give your in-laws time to adjust to this fact. Your fiancé's mother has been close to your fiancé for many years. Recognize that the process of separation should be as gradual as possible.

If you want to give advice to your future in-laws, it is usually best to wait until they ask for it. If you offer a suggestion to them, remember that they have the right to accept or reject it. After all, don't you want the same right?

Don't discuss your disagreements and your future spouse's faults with your family. If you do you may bias them against your fiancé, thus making it more difficult for all parties involved to achieve a better relationship.

Don't quote your family or hold them up as models to your

fiancé. He/she will probably feel defensive and seek to defend his/her own parents' way of doing things, even if you are correct in your statements. If you desire your future in-laws to do something differently, ask your fiancé how he/she feels about his/her parents. Perhaps he/she can share some insights about their behavior that you cannot see. Remember that both families have their idiosyncrasies and eccentricities. This is called being human!

1. What have you done in the past to let both your own parents and your future in-laws know they are important to you?

2. During the past two weeks, what have you done to express your positive feelings toward your parents and your future in-laws?

3. What additional things could you say or do that would let your parents and future in-laws know they are important to you?

4. What have you learned about the kind of relationship your parents or future in-laws expect from you and your fiancé? (Such as how often to visit or call, their involvement in disciplining your children, etc.)

   What should you do about their expectations in the future?

5. In the past, how have you helped your parents meet their own needs and develop a greater meaning in life?

How can you help them in the future?

6. If your parents have had serious difficulties in the past, how did you respond to them?

How can you be more helpful in the future?

7. In the past, what have you done with your parents or future in-laws to make it easier for them to demonstrate love toward you and your fiancé?

How can you improve this in the future?

8. What have you done in the past to assist your parents or prospective in-laws to receive love from you? What have you done to demonstrate love to them?

COMMITMENT TO FORGIVE AND PRAY TOGETHER

"Is there any special ingredient that will help us have a consistent and growing marriage?" couples often ask. Yes, there is! Naturally all that we have talked about is important, but there are two other areas which, if mastered and practiced in your marriage, will give you the depth and stability you are seeking. These are forgiveness and praying together.

The First Ingredient

Listen to the words of a husband who has been married for several years:

> When we got married, no one could have predicted what would happen in the next few years. I guess no one knows what will happen; if they did, fewer people would marry. I guess I still have hope because of my Christian faith. I just pray that we will find a way to turn back to the Lord and let His love and forgiveness heal the wounds and scars of our marriage. Forgiveness—that's a hard word. I wish someone had taught us more about that before we married. That's a word we're just beginning to learn about.

If you love another person you must be willing to run the risk of being hurt. Hurt brings pain, but through hurt comes the opportunity for forgiveness and reconciliation. Is forgiveness easy for you? Is it available to you? Have you experienced the process of forgiving others and being forgiven?

Many marriages are gradually eroded and eventually destroyed because one person is unable to forgive. A person who continually brings up something his spouse did or said in the past that was hurtful to himself continues to punish the other person and erects a wall of indifference and coldness.

If we know Jesus Christ as Saviour, we have experienced God's forgiveness. Because we are in Christ we have the capacity to forgive ourselves and thus are enabled to forgive others. Paul spoke to us directly on this account: "Be gentle and forbearing with one another and, if one has a difference (a grievance or complaint) against another, readily pardoning each other; even as the Lord has freely forgiven you, so must you also [forgive]" (Col. 3:13, *AMP*).

What True Forgiveness *Is Not*

More than any other people, Christians have the capacity to forgive. What is forgiveness? What is it not? Perhaps one of the best ways to discover what forgiveness is, is to consider what it is not.

Forgiveness is not forgetting. God constructed you in such a way that your brain is like a giant computer. Whatever has happened to you is stored in your memory. The remembrance will always be with you. There are, however, two different ways of remembering. One is to recall the offense or hurt in such a way that it continues to affect you and your relationship with another. It continues to eat away and bother you so that the hurt remains. Another way of remembering, however, simply says, "Yes, that happened. I know it did, but it no longer affects me. It's a fact of history, yet it has no emotional significance or effect. It's there, but we are progressing onward at this time and I am not hindered nor is our relationship hurt by that event." This is, in a sense, forgetting. The fact remains, but it no longer entangles you in its tentacles of control.

Forgiveness is not pretending. You cannot ignore the fact that an event occurred. Wishing it never happened will not make it go away. What has been done is done. Becoming a martyr and pretending ignorance of the event does not help the relationship. In fact, your lack of confrontation and reconciliation may encourage the other person to continue or repeat the same act or behavior.

Forgiveness is not a feeling. It is a clear and logical action on your part. It is not a soothing, comforting, overwhelming emotional response that erases the fact from your memory forever.

Forgiveness is not bringing up the past. It is so easy to bring up past offenses and hurts. There are some who have a trading-stamp book with unlimited pages. For each hurt they lick a stamp and paste it in. When the right time comes, they cash in those pages. Bringing up the past is destructive because:

- There is nothing you can do to change it.
- It takes you away from giving your energy to the present and future.
- It makes you responsible at this point for jeopardizing the marriage.
- Even if you were severely offended, by dwelling on the offense you place a continuing burden on your marriage.
- It denies your partner the opportunity to change for the better. This behavior also denies the presence and power of the person of Jesus Christ in a life!
- It does little to elevate you in the eyes of others.

An indication of maturity is the desire and willingness to break loose of the past and move forward.

Forgiveness is not demanding change before you forgive. If you demand a change or demand proof of it first, you expose your own faithlessness and unwillingness to believe in the other person. He/she has already changed in a sense by coming and asking for forgiveness. The change is in his/her heart, but do you really trust that change?

Often, instead of complete forgiveness, we say, "I'll have to wait and see" or "Give me time." Time is often involved because forgiveness is a process and often does not occur instantaneously. You have to work through your feelings. But are you working through your feelings by yourself or waiting for definite signs of change on the part of the other person?

You don't want to risk being hurt again, so you are cautious and distrustful. This approach puts you in the role of a judge. The other person's change of heart has to be proved to you and maybe your criteria of proof is so subjective that he/she can never measure up.

When forgiveness is lacking a strange bedfellow by the name of bitterness creeps in. Another word for bitterness is poison. It is poison both to the person possessing it and to the relationship. The Word of God says, "Let there be no more bitterness" (see Eph. 4:31). Bitterness means that we have the desire to get even. But getting even costs. It can cost us in our bodies— ulcerative colitis, toxic goiter, high blood pressure, ulcers. These are just a few of the by-products.

What True Forgiveness *Is*

Forgiveness is rare because it is hard. It will cost you love and pride. To forgive means giving up defending yourself. It means not allowing the other person to pay. It repudiates revenge and does not demand its rights. Perhaps we could say that it involves suffering.

> *Forgiveness is self-giving:* It gives love where the enemy expects hatred. It gives freedom where the enemy deserves punishment. It gives understanding where the enemy anticipates anger and revenge. Forgiveness refuses to seek its own advantage. It gives back to the person his freedom and his future.[1]
>
> *Forgiveness is costly and is substitutional:* All forgiveness, human and divine, is in the very nature of the case vicarious, substitutional, and this is one of the most valuable views my mind has ever entertained. No one ever really forgives another, except he hears the penalty of the other's sin against him.[2]

Our greatest example of forgiveness is the cross of Jesus Christ. God chose the cross as the way of reconciliation. "For you have been called for this purpose, since Christ also suffered for you, leaving you an example for you to follow in His steps" (1

Pet. 2:21, *NASB*). "He himself bore our sins . . . on the tree" (1 Pet. 2:24, *RSV*). And we are called to forgive as God has forgiven us. "Be as ready to forgive others as God for Christ's sake has forgiven you" (Eph. 4:32, *Phillips*).

Forgiveness takes place when love accepts—deliberately—the hurts and abrasions of life and drops all charges against the other person. Forgiveness is accepting the other when both of you know he or she has done something quite unacceptable.

Forgiveness is smiling silent love to your partner when the justifications for keeping an insult or injury alive are on the tip of your tongue, yet you swallow them. Not because you have to, to keep peace, but because you want to, to make peace.

Forgiveness is not acceptance given "on condition" that the other become acceptable. Forgiveness is given freely. Out of the keen awareness that the forgiver also has a need of constant forgiveness, daily.

Forgiveness exercises God's strength to love and receives the other person without any assurance of complete restitution and making of amends.

Forgiveness is a relationship between equals who recognize their need of each other, share and share alike. Each needs the other's forgiveness. Each needs the other's acceptance. Each needs the other. And so, before God, each drops all charges, refuses all self-justification, and forgives. And forgives. Seventy times seven. As Jesus said.[3]

The Second Ingredient

The first ingredient, then, for a consistent, growing marriage is forgiveness. The second ingredient is prayer. Praying together as a couple can be a highlight of your courtship and marriage. Often we think of romantic interludes, a special trip together or a night of sexual ecstasy as the peak experiences of marriage. They can be. But right along with these, and perhaps even surpassing them, can be the times of praying together. There is a special closeness and intimacy that can develop as each person opens his/her inner self and soul to the Lord and to one another through the avenue of praying to God.

Do not wait until you are married to begin this adventure together. The best time to begin is while you are engaged. Praying to the Lord together can be a reminder of your responsibility to follow His directives in Scripture and causes you to consider those areas of your marriage which may not fully reflect His Word.

The majority of Christian couples do *not* have this special element as a part of their relationship. I'm sure there are many reasons why they do not. Perhaps some of those reasons are why you may be hesitant to pray together.

How many of us have ever been taught how to pray together as a couple? How many of us have any models of couples who pray together regularly and are willing to share with us what they learned and how prayer has drawn them closer together in their relationship?

Often one of the partners wants to pray but the other is hesitant. Perhaps the partner is not accustomed to praying out loud and because of comparing himself/herself to the other feels very inadequate. Or he/she has never developed a personal prayer life and communicating with God is foreign to him/her. You may feel that you must pray together every day at least 15 or 20 minutes. Because of the hectic pace of your lives, it is difficult to achieve this, so nothing happens.

Praying together is a time of coming together in the presence of God. There is no "right" amount of time to spend praying. Often couples begin by taking a minute or two to share concerns and requests. Then they pray silently together. After establishing this practice they may feel comfortable praying aloud together. Some couples take a brief time after a date to share and pray. They pray for each other at specific times during the day as well. Other couples pray at the evening meal. The idea is to establish a pattern of prayer for your lives together. Some couples read a book together on the subject of prayer or, as Joyce and I have done, read aloud the daily reading from Lloyd

Ogilvie's book, *God's Best for Today.*

I have always liked what Paul Tournier and Dwight Small have to say about prayer in a couple's life. Consider their words as you contemplate incorporating prayer into your relationship.

> It is only when a husband and wife pray together before God that they find the secret of true harmony, that the difference in their temperaments, their ideas, and their tastes enriches their home instead of endangering it. There will be no further question of one imposing his will on the other, or of the other giving in for the sake of peace. Instead, they will together seek God's will, which alone will ensure that each will be fully able to develop his personality . . . When each of the marriage partners seeks quietly before God to see his own faults, recognizes his sin, and asks the forgiveness of the other, marital problems are no more. Each learns to speak the other's language, and to meet him halfway, so to speak. Each holds back those harsh little words which one is apt to utter when one is right, but which are said in order to injure. Most of all, a couple rediscovers complete mutual confidence, because, in meditating in prayer together, they learn to become absolutely honest with each other . . . . This is the price to be paid if partners very different from each other are to combine their gifts instead of setting them against each other.[4]

> Lines open to God are invariably open to one another for a person cannot be genuinely open to God and closed to his mate. Praying together especially reduces the sense of complementarity and completeness. The Holy Spirit seeks only the opportunity to minister to whatever needs are present in a marriage, and in their moments of prayer together a couple give Him entrance into opened hearts and minds. God fulfills His design for Christian marriage when lines of communication are first opened to Him.[5]

If you would like open lines of communication, begin to pray together now as a couple.

As you begin your marriage, you are starting to accumulate memories. What will make the difference in the quality of your memories?

One word—commitment.

One word? Yes, but a costly word that can bring tension and questions at the same time can bring peace, maturity and stability.

In the midst of a life that brings rapid, unexpected changes, unfairness, tragedy and unanswered questions, commitment to living by faith will guide you through this journey.

Commit your life to the person of Jesus Christ who is the Son of God.

Commit your life to the Word of God which brings stability and peace.

Commit yourself to seeing your future spouse as having such worth, value and dignity that God sent His Son to die for that person.

Commit your life as a couple to a life of prayer. There is no greater closeness and intimacy than when a couple opens their hearts to God together. Praying together enhances the completeness and oneness of a couple while it puts their differences and adjustments in a better perspective.

Commit your life to giving your marriage top priority in terms of time, energy, thought and planning for growth.

Commit yourself to a life of fidelity and faithfulness regardless of your feelings or the lure of life around you.

Commit and open yourself to the working of the Holy Spirit in your life. "But when the Holy Spirit controls our lives he will produce this kind of fruit in us: love, joy, peace, patience, kindness, goodness, faithfulness, gentleness and self-control" (Gal. 5:22-23, *TLB*).

Faith, hope and love will grow out of your commitment to one another and to God and His Word. May the following always be *your* prayer:

Lord, we believe that You ordained marriage

and that You also sustain it.
Help us to exercise faith.
>Faith that You answer prayer
>>and heal wounded hearts.
>Faith that You Forgive and restore.
>Faith that Your hand of love
>>will clasp our hands together.
>Faith that You build bridges of reconciliation.
>Faith that all things will work for good
>>to those who love You.

Help us to hold on to hope.
>Hope that enables us to endure
>>times of trial and testing.

Hope that fixes our gaze on possibilities
>rather than problems.

Hope that focuses on the road ahead
>instead of detours already passed.
>Hope that instills trust, even in the midst of failure.
>Hope that harbors happiness.

Help us to lift up love.
>Love that doesn't falter or faint
>>in the winds of adversity.
>Love that is determined to grow and bear fruit.
>Love that is slow to anger and quick to praise.
>Love that looks for ways of saying
>>"I care for you."
>Love that remains steady during shaky days.

Lord, may Your gifts of faith, hope and love find plenty of living room in our hearts. Thank You that these three abide—and the greatest is love. Make our home an outpost for Your kingdom and an oasis for wandering pilgrims. In the name of Jesus who blessed the marriage at Cana with a miracle. Amen.[6]

NOTES

Chapter 1

1. From H.L. Silverman, ed., *Marital Therapy: Psychological, Sociological and Moral Factors*, 1972. Courtesy of Charles C Thomas, Publisher, Springfield, Illinois.

2. David Knox, *Marriage: Who? When? Why?* (Englewood Cliffs, NJ: Prentice Hall, Inc., 1974).

3. MARRIAGE AT ITS BEST by John Lavender © 1982, Accent Publications, Inc., Denver, CO. Used with permission.

4. David and Vera Mace, *We Can Have Better Marriages If We Really Want Them* (Nashville: Abingdon Press, 1974), p. 98.

5. David Augsburger, *Cherishable Love and Marriage* (Scottdale, PA: Herald Press, 1971), p. 97. Used with permission.

6. Lavender, MARRIAGE AT ITS BEST. Used with permission of Accent Publications, Inc.

7. Dwight H. Small, *Marriage As Equal Partnership* (Grand Rapids: Baker Book House, 1980), pp. 29-30, 48. Used with permission.

8. Taken from *How Do You Say, "I Love You"?* by Judson Swihart. © 1977 by Inter-Varsity Christian Fellowship of the USA and used with permission.

9. Lewis B. Smedes, *How Can It Be All Right When Everything Is All Wrong?* (San Francisco: Harper & Row Publishers, Inc., 1982), p. 61.

10. For additional information, read chapters 1 and 6 in *Before You Say I Do* by Wes Roberts and H. Norman Wright, published by Harvest House Publishers.

Chapter 2

1. Hugh Missildine, *Your Inner Child of the Past* (New York: Simon and Schuster, 1963), p. 59.

2. Howard Halpern, *Cutting Loose: A Guide to Adult Terms with Your Parents* (New York: Bantam Books, Inc., 1978), p. 3.

Chapter 3

1. From GETTING CONTROL OF YOUR INNER SELF by Rick Yohn, published by Tyndale House Publishers, © 1982 by Rick Yohn. Used by permission.

2. Eric Fromm, as quoted in Leo Buscaglia, *Love* (Thorofare, NJ: Charles B. Slack, Inc., 1972), p. 66.

3. Lewis B. Smedes, *Love Within Limits* (Grand Rapids: Wm. B. Eerdmans Publishing Co., 1978), p. 63. Used by permission.

4. Paul Tournier, *Secrets* (Richmond, VA: John Knox Press, 1965), p. 50. Used with permission.

5. Dwight Small, *How Should I Love You?* (New York: Harper & Row Publishers, Inc., 1979).

6. Walter Trobisch, *I Married You* (New York: Harper & Row Publishers, Inc., 1975), pp. 75-77.

7. William J. McRae, *Preparing for Your Marriage* (Grand Rapids: Zondervan Publishing House, 1980), p. 37.

8. Jerry and Barbara Cook, *Choosing to Love* (Ventura, CA: Regal Books, 1982), pp. 18-19. Used by permission.

9. For additional study, complete chapter 3 of *Before You Say I Do* by Wes Roberts and Norman Wright.

Chapter 4

1. David and Vera Mace, *We Can Have Better Marriages If We Really Want Them* (Nashville: Abingdon Press, 1974), p. 9.

2. Robert Mason, Jr. and Caroline L. Jacobs, *How to Choose the Wrong Marriage Partner and Live Unhappily Ever After* (Atlanta: John Knox Press, 1979), p. 40. Used by permission.

3. Clark Blackburn and Norman Lobsenz, *How to Stay Married* (New York: Cowles Books, 1968), p. 196.

4. Arthur J. Snider, "25 Most Distressing Events in Your Life," *Science Digest,* May, 1971, pp. 68-72.

5. Mark Lee, *Time Bombs in Marriage* (Chappaqwa, NY: Christian Herald Association, 1981), p. 10. Used by permission.

6. Diane de Dubovay and Robert Redford, "Robert Redford," *Ladies Home Journal,* October, 1981, pp. 48,52.

Chapter 5

1. Excerpt from UNFINISHED BUSINESS by Maggie Scarf. © 1980 by Maggie Scarf. Reprinted by permission of Doubleday & Company, Inc. .

2. Daniel Levinson, *The Seasons of a Man's Life* (New York: Alfred A. Knopf, Inc., 1978), p. 71. Used by permission.

3. Material in this section was adapted from both Scarf, *Unfinished Business* and Levinson, *The Seasons of a Man's Life.*

4. Mel Krantzler, *Creative Marriage* (New York: McGraw-Hill Book Co., 1981), p. 50. Used by permission.

5. Ibid., p. 54. Used by permission.

6. Jane Aldous, *Family Careers—Developmental Change in Families* (New York: John Wiley, 1978), p. 202. Used by permission.

7. Adapted from Marvin H. Inmon and H. Norman Wright, *Preparing for Parenthood* (Ventura, CA: Regal Books, 1980). Used by permission.

8. Krantzler, *Creative Marriage*, pp. 67-73. More information on this subject is in G. Wade Rowatt, Jr. and Mary Jo Rowatt, *The Two-Career Marriage* (Philadelphia: Westminster Press, 1980); Caroline Bird, *The Paycheck Marraige* (New York: Rawson, Wade Publishers, Inc., 1979).

9. Lloyd H. Ahlem, *Do I Have to Be Me?* (Ventura, CA: Regal Books, 1973), p. 64. Used by permission.

Chapter 6

1. Phillip Yancy, *After the Wedding* (Waco, TX: Word Books, 1976), pp. 29-30.

2. Abraham Schmitt, "Conflict and Ecstacy—Model for Maturing Marriage," an original paper.

3. Nick Stinnett, Barbara Chesser and John DeFrain, eds., *Building Family Strengths: Blueprint for Action* (Lincoln, NB: University of Nebraska Press, 1979), p. 112. Used by permission.

4. Reprinted with permission of The Free Press, a Division of Macmillan, Inc. from *A Strategy for Daily Living* by Ari Kiev. Copyright © 1973 by Ari Kiev, M.D.

5. Adapted from Edward R. Dayton and Ted W. Engstrom, *Strategy for Living* (Ventura, CA: Regal Books, 1976), pp. 55-56. Used by permission.

Chapter 7

1. Don Jackson and Richard Lederer, *The Mirages of Marriage* (New York: W.W. Norton & Co., 1968), pp. 248-249.

2. H. Norman Wright, *The Family that Listens* (Wheaton, IL: Scripture Press, 1978), pp. 32-33. Used by permission.

3. Chuck Gallagher, *Love Is a Couple* (New York: Sadlier Publishers, 1976), pp. 76-77. Used by permission.

4. Louis Evans, Jr., and Colleen Evans, "Gifts of the Spirit in Marriage," as quoted in Gary Collins, ed., *Make More of Your Marriage* (Waco, TX: Word Books, 1976), pp. 38-39.

5. Excerpt from NO FAULT MARRIAGE by Marcia Laswell and Norman M. Lobsenz. Copyright © 1976 by Marcia Laswell and Norman M. Lopsenz. Reprinted by permission of Doubleday & Company, Inc. .

6. Ibid., p. 221. Used by permission.

7. James Jauncey, *Magic in Marriage* (Waco, TX: Word Books, 1968), pp. 126-127.

Chapter 8

1. Reuel Howe, *The Miracle of Dialogue* (New York: Seabury Press, 1963), p. 3.

2. Reuel Howe, *Herein Is Love* (Valley Forge, PA: Judson Press, 1961), p. 100. Used by permission of Judson Press.

3. Mark Lee, "Why Marriages Fail—Communication," in Gary Collins, ed., *Make More of Your Marriage* (Waco, TX: Word Books, 1976), p. 75.

4. Adapted from Jerry Richardson and Joel Margulis, *The Magic of Rapport* (San

Francisco: Harbor Publishing, 1981).

5. For a detailed Bible study on communication, complete chapter 9 of the book *Before You Say I Do* by Wes Roberts and H. Norman Wright, published by Harvest House Publishers.

Chapter 9

1. From TOUGH AND TENDER by Joyce Landorf, copyright © 1975, 1981 by Fleming H. Revell Company. Used by permission.

2. David Augsburger, *Caring Enough to Hear* (Ventura, CA: Regal Books, 1982), pp. 41-42. Used by permission.

3. Ibid. Used by permission.

Chapter 10

1. Warren Farrell, *The Liberated Man* (New York: Random House, Inc., 1974), pp. 328-329.

2. Herb Goldberg, *The Hazards of Being Male* (New York: The New American Library, 1975), p. 39.

Chapter 11

1. James G.T. Fairfield, *When You Don't Agree* (Scottdale, PA: Herald Press, 1977), p. 18. Used by permission.

2. David and Vera Mace, *We Can Have Better Marriages If We Really Want Them* (Nashville: Abingdon Press, 1974), pp. 88-90.

3. Fairfield, *When You Don't Agree*, p. 19. Used by permission.

4. From AFTER YOU'VE SAID 'I DO' by Dwight Harvey Small, copyright © 1968 by Fleming H. Revell, Company. Used by permission.

5. Ibid., p. 130. Used by permission.

6. Taken from EVERYTHING YOU NEED TO KNOW TO STAY MARRIED AND LIKE IT, by Bennard Wiese and Urban Steinmetz. Copyright © 1972 by Bennard R. Wiese. Used by permission of Zondervan Publishing House.

7. Small, *After You've Said I Do*, p. 139. Used by permission.

8. © 1977 Gladys Hunt. Published by David C. Cook Publishing Co., Elgin, IL

60120. Used by permission.

9. Fairfield, *When You Don't Agree*, p. 9. Used by permission.

10. Mace, *We Can Have Better Marriages*, p. 89.

11. Ibid.

12. Roy W. Fairchild, *Christians in Families* (Atlanta: John Knox Press, 1964), pp. 169-170. Used by permission.

Chapter 12

1. David Burns, M.D. *Feeling Good: The New Mood Therapy* (New York: New American Library, Inc., 1980), p. 152.

2. Joseph R. Cooke, *Free for the Taking* (Old Tappan, NJ: Fleming H. Revell Co., 1975), pp. 109-110. Used by permission.

3. David R. Mace, "Marital Intimacy and the Deadly Love-Anger Cycle," *Journal of Marriage and Family Counseling*, April 1976, p. 136.

4. Taken from ANGER: YOURS & MINE & WHAT TO DO ABOUT IT, by Richard P. Walters. Copyright © 1981 by The Zondervan Publishing Corporation. Used by permission.

Chapter 14

1. From *Freedom of Forgiveness* by David Augsburger. Copyright © 1970. Moody Press. Moody Bible Institute of Chicago. Used by permission.

2. James O. Buswell, Jr., *A Systematic Theology of Christian Religion* (Grand Rapids: Zondervan Publishing House, 1962), p. 276.

3. David Augsburger, *Cherishable Love and Marriage* (Harrisonburg, VA: Herald Press, 1976), p. 146. Used by permission.

4. Paul Tournier, *The Healing of Persons* (New York: Harper & Row Publishers, 1965), pp. 88-89.

5. From AFTER YOU'VE SAID 'I DO' by Dwight Harvey Small, copyright © 1968 by Fleming H. Revell Company. Used by permission.

6. Reprinted by permission from FORTY WAYS TO SAY I LOVE YOU by James R. Bjorge, copyright 1978 Augsburg Publishing House.